THE NATURE OF GOD IN PLAIN LANGUAGE

David L. Hocking

WORD BOOKS
PUBLISHER
WACO, TEXAS

A DIVISION OF
WORD, INCORPORATED

Library of Congress Cataloging in Publication Data

Hocking, David L.
   The nature of God in plain language.

   Bibliography: p.
   1. God. I. Title.
   BT102.H58   1984   231   84-7210
   ISBN 0-8499-0428-5

To My Parents

who first taught me about God and instilled a love for His attributes and ways by their example and concern for me

Contents

Foreword

Theology has a mystique about it. Unusual thoughts come to mind when people hear this term. To some theology has the aura of antiquity—a medieval monk hovering over a dusty manuscript in a dimly lit room. To others it suggests an academic environment—a professor in the midst of pious young men enthralled by words and phrases unknown to the average crowd. Dr. Hocking has brought theology into everyday life. It is not only clothed in plain language so it can be understood, it is also set in the arena of our work-a-day world and shown to be full of meaning and spiritual help for every Christian.

This book answers basic questions about God. Does God exist? If so, where? Is He real? How powerful is He? Can I know Him, and is He really interested in me? The genius of the book is that Dr. Hocking explains the nature of God in everyday terms. He skillfully weaves together doctrine with down-to-earth illustrations.

Profound truth is expressed informally and warmly. The reader may feel that he is sitting with the author in his home, listening to personal experiences. Sometimes it is as if one is worshiping with Dr. Hocking's congregation. The scholar is also seen at work in his study—tracing the meaning of a word in the original language, or reflecting upon a thought from an established creed.

This book reflects the fact that the author is well acquainted with the standard theologies. There are no surprises. His handling of the material about God is very credible. The many quotes and references from the Scripture allow this volume to be valuable as a study guide. This is not one man's musing about God. Rather it is a treatise based on the biblical revelation of God.

The practical value of the book is best seen in the last four chapters, which deal with God's power, His knowledge, His trustworthiness, and His care for us. Here is theology in action. God is not just someone "way out there" who has little interest in the world; God is involved in all of His creation. His presence helps us in every situation from day to day.

Dr. Hocking is to be commended for his endeavor to make us more aware of God and God's significance in life. This book is not exhaustive, but it will motivate believers to continue to pursue the knowledge of the Most High.

DR. WENDELL G. JOHNSTON
Dean of Talbot Theological Seminary and School of Theology

Introduction

Printed on all the coins we use in America are the words "IN GOD WE TRUST." Whenever we give the Pledge of Allegiance to our country, we say, "ONE NATION UNDER GOD." On the fourth of July each year, we celebrate Independence Day, reminding us of the signing of the Declaration of Independence. We hear many songs that speak of patriotism and love of country, and we sing "God Bless America" and "America the Beautiful," in which we say, "America! America! God Shed His Grace on Thee."

Most Americans, according to surveys of recent years, believe in the existence of God. But when it comes down to describing Him, we get a little hesitant, defensive, or just plain confused. The big question remains—WHO IS GOD?

Life is filled with many questions. Where did we come from? Why are we here? Where are we going? What about suffering, sickness, death, life after death, and so on? Is there a God? What is He like? Can we know Him in a personal way, as we know each other? If He really exists, why doesn't He do something about the mess we are in? Why doesn't He straighten things out? Does He care? Maybe God is a little like Santa Claus or the Easter Bunny—a harmless fantasy for little children, but not believable for mature adults!

The logical place to which most people turn in their search for God is religious teaching—a local church, synagogue, or any number of religious organizations and schools. What do we find?

Lots of opinions and many disagreements. God means different things to different people. When you study the religions of the world and the sacred writings they produce, you once again discover the multitude of ideas about God, as to who He is, and what He can do. But which group is right? Whom do we believe and why should we believe it?

Ancient Greece and Rome had many ideas about God. Many of their gods had feet of clay and did as much evil as they did good. They seemed more like people than gods. Polytheism was tolerated because no one could agree. Freedom of religion meant that you could believe whatever you wanted to, as long as you were loyal to the state. Athens, Greece, was a great center for religious ideas and concepts about God. According to the Bible (Acts 17), Athens even had an altar dedicated "TO THE UN-KNOWN GOD." Presumably that would cover any god they might have missed in their discussions! In one sense, it seems ironic that such an altar existed. One of the early leaders of Christianity, an incredibly brilliant and well-educated man named Paul, referred to that altar in Athens and the God it represented with these words:

> "Therefore, the One whom you worship without knowing, Him I proclaim to you: God, who made the world and everything in it, since He is Lord of heaven and earth, does not dwell in temples made with hands. Nor is He worshiped with men's hands, as though He needed anything, since He gives to all life, breath, and all things. And He has made from one blood every nation of men to dwell on all the face of the earth, and has determined their preappointed times and the boundaries of their habitation, so that they should seek the Lord, in the hope that they might grope for Him and find Him, though He is not far from each one of us; for in Him we live and move and have our being, as also some of your own poets have said, 'For we are also His offspring.' Therefore, since we are the offspring of God, we ought not to think that the Divine Nature is like gold or silver or stone, something shaped by art and man's devising."

> Acts 17:23–29

Let's face it—God is the great "Unknown" to many of us. We want to believe that He exists, but He seems unknowable and impersonal to most of us.

While vacationing in Palm Springs for a few days, my wife and I encountered a Jewish man who seemed interested in knowing God. He had never denied the presence and existence of God, but God seemed quite remote to him, and he wanted to know if it was possible to know God in a personal way. We talked for quite some time about who God is and what He is like. This man told me that most of his life was lived around materialistic goals, and he frankly saw little need for God in his life. But now that he was getting older, he was becoming more concerned. He was amazed at some of the things we shared with him and wanted to know more. I realized then the need and importance of a book that would talk about God in plain language—so that everyone could understand and get some of the basic questions answered.

It seems to me that in moments of heartache, disappointment, and discouragement, most of us would like to know if there is a God who understands our feelings and cares about us. When your total perspective in life begins and ends with self, there is very little comfort and hope. When your dreams are shattered, your ideals destroyed, and your goals unrealized, a certain emptiness remains that only God can fill. The big questions about the origin of all things, death, and life after death are answered satisfactorily only when we root our understanding in the presence and existence of God, a God who knows the beginning and the end of all things and who is personally involved in the course of human lives and events. I believe that such a God really exists and that He is personal and knowable. This book is dedicated to introducing you to the "ONE AND ONLY GOD."

DAVID L. HOCKING

THE NATURE OF GOD IN PLAIN LANGUAGE

1

Does God Really Exist?

As I was waiting to play racquetball at a YMCA in a city where I was speaking, a young teenage girl came up to me and started telling me her life story. I stopped her after a few minutes and asked, "Why are you telling me all of this?" She said, "I just wanted someone to talk to, and you looked like you would listen!" She was raised in a home where it was demanded that you believe in God, but there was no evidence in her parents that it made any difference. They were alcoholics and had rid themselves of her when she was just fifteen years old. She fell into the drug scene and various sexual encounters until she felt abused, lonely, bitter, and suicidal. She had been arrested for drug abuse and was now in an institution that was designed to help her. Her real problem was the existence of God. She had a difficult time believing that there was a God who really cared about her. She had been told that God existed and was even sent to church when she was a child. But her heart was restless and dissatisfied—the vacuum was still there, and only a personal, loving God could fill it. It was a great privilege for me that day to tell her about the God who loves her and cares about her life and problems.

Why Do Some People Not Believe There Is a God?

Like that teenage girl, some of us doubt there is a God because those who say that they believe in Him show no evidence in their lives that it makes one bit of difference. Belief in the existence of God seems to have little effect upon what some people think, say, or do. In a certain respect, they are "closet atheists." They would never admit that they do not believe in the existence of God, but their lifestyle, priorities, and attitudes often reveal the opposite. They live as if He does not exist, since they pay no attention to His presence or authority over them.

When I asked a salesman about the existence of God, he said, "Of course I believe in God, but I don't want Him telling me what to do!" Unfortunately, this salesman was more interested in selling me his product than in hearing what I had to say about the presence and existence of God. He had no personal relationship or response to the God he said he believed in, because he did not want to be accountable to that God for his actions. He wanted to run his own life, and he didn't want to know about a God to whom he might be responsible.

Because they see no evidence (at least from their perspective) that God exists, many people do not believe in Him. They think that some people believe in God only because they have failed to cope with life or some personal problem. They see God as a crutch for people to depend on in a difficult situation. That's what a fifty-five-year-old military man told me. He saw God as something which little children, women, and helpless people need. He was self-confident (and a little arrogant) and did not see his need for God, much less believe that such a God really exists.

A gas station attendant told me, "If there is a God, there's no way you can prove it." He told me about the Russian cosmonaut who traveled far into space and said that there was no sign of God anywhere!

Some people with whom I have talked about God seem to know one thing: That you can't know if there is a God or not! They seem to ignore the fact that we are often ignorant of what others may know. This agnostic attitude is understandable. Our struggle with the unknown may cause us at times to deny that something exists, simply because we cannot see it or understand it. I believe in electricity, but I have never seen it. If you stick a wet finger in a socket, however, it might make you a believer!

One college student told me that he had tried to discover who God is, but simply came "to a dead-end street." After taking some classes at the local university in his city dealing with the religions of the world, he came to the conclusion that it is impossible to know who God is. He was frustrated and disillusioned.

One man's doubts are another man's beliefs. Experience often makes the difference. When the facts you say you believe do not bring any positive and observable results in your experience, you begin to question the validity of those facts. I have often encountered believers in God who fall into this category, simply because they see no concrete evidence of God's existence and work in their lives. They are afraid to deny His existence, but in their hearts, they doubt it.

Some People Don't Think They Need God!

In a materialistic culture as we have here in America, our "security blanket" is often found in the things that we possess. This gives us a feeling of self-worth and importance, and we relate more to the physical and material than the spiritual and unseen. In times of material prosperity, it is natural to feel that we do not need God. We are getting along just fine without Him—or so we think!

Jewish people are aware of the dangers which material prosperity places upon our belief in God. In the Book of Deuteronomy, the people of Israel are told by Moses:

> "Beware that you do not forget the LORD your God by not keeping His commandments, His judgments, and His statutes which I command you today, lest—when you have eaten and are full, and have built beautiful houses and dwelt in them; and when your herds and your flocks multiply, and your silver and your gold are multiplied, and all that you have is multiplied; when your heart is lifted up, and you forget the LORD your God. . . ."
>
> Deuteronomy 8:11–14

Many people follow a materialistic viewpoint because they know that life is short and they want to enjoy it while they can.

They usually concentrate on "things" and the so-called pleasures of life. These people are usually not concerned about God and eternal issues until some tragedy or circumstance removes their reason for living. When they have nowhere to turn, and the things they have accumulated no longer satisfy, they are often open to the truth about the existence and plan of God.

Jesus Christ taught us the danger of materialism. He pointed out that the materialist places more value on temporal things than eternal things. He said that a man who lays up treasures for himself is a fool (Luke 12:19–21). When death comes, he cannot take these with him. Jesus also said that a man's life does not consist of the abundance of his possessions. The materialist believes his life has value when he accumulates "things," but these do not bring happiness. Some of the world's most unhappy people are to be found among the very rich. The materialist fails to recognize the source of all he possesses. His ability to work, earn money, and acquire things is a gift from God.

Many of us are blind to our own needs. We may think that we do not need God, but sooner or later we will discover differently that we do. The greater our reliance upon things, the less we feel the need to depend upon God. One wealthy gentleman put it to me this way: "What could God possibly give me that I don't already have?" My answer: "Eternal life." That gentleman decided that what I had to say was worth hearing now. He listened quietly as I told him about the one and only God and the conditions for experiencing eternal life. One thing is sure—you can't take your "things" with you when you die. They will not help you to face eternity or even your own death!

Which Religion Is Correct?

A lot of evil has been done in the name of religion. Although most of the peoples of the world believe in the existence of God, they disagree about who He is and what He can do or will do. Some religious teaching has resulted in great harm because it has often led people astray and been oblivious to the facts. It has shown disregard for human life and property and has often "convinced" people to believe at the point of a sword. Galileo was accused of heresy because he believed that the earth revolved around the sun. The people of Jonestown were persuaded to commit mass suicide as an honorable and God-pleasing act. Hitler used religion to manipulate people's viewpoints and attitudes toward the Jewish people. In the name of religion and the honor of God, many wars have been started and thousands of lives destroyed.

If religious beliefs in God have led to so much suffering and tragedy, how can we have confidence in what religious leaders tell us or their books try to prove? Each religion is fully confident that its sacred writings are the real truth about God. Jews turn to the Bible as Christians do, although Christians add the books of the New Testament. Roman Catholics have a few more books in their Bible than the Protestants accept. Muslims turn to the Koran, and Mormons believe in the Book of Mormon, *Doctrines and Covenants, Pearl of Great Price,* and so on. The writings of Confucius, Buddha, and the great thinkers of the Hindus are all dedicated to helping us understand the existence and presence of God. The number of cults, isms, and religious beliefs in the world is staggering—which one is correct?

Some argue for the existence of God simply *because* there are so many religious viewpoints in the world today. They speak of the "universal idea of God" in the heart of every man and see this as clear evidence that there is a God. To them, it appears that there is a God-shaped vacuum in the heart of every one of us that can be filled only by God Himself. An interesting view! But again, which viewpoint do we follow?

However, the very fact that there are so many viewpoints and opinions about God has led other people to question the possibility of ever knowing for sure that God really exists. Many of us are frustrated by our differences, and we give up the struggle to find out for ourselves. When so many people disagree, how can anyone know for sure that he or she is right? A friend of mine who is a pastor of a very large church says, "I know I'm right. If I weren't, I would change my view!" We smile at that, and so does he. It only brings out our basic problem: We all want to be right, and it is hard for us to admit that we may be wrong. Pride often stands in the way—it keeps us from pursuing more knowledge or learning from others what we ourselves have never discovered.

Consider the Facts!

An old television program called "Dragnet," starring Jack Webb as a Los Angeles police officer, had him saying to people whom he was questioning concerning a crime: "Just the facts, ma'am, just the facts!" That is the kind of investigation that is needed if we are going to discover the possibility of God's existence. Those facts that have made an impression on me may not affect you in the same way, but it may help us all to take another look at them.

The facts that lead me to believe in the existence of a personal God include:

1. The existence of the material universe
2. The order and design of the universe
3. The nature of man
4. The reliability and accuracy of the Bible
5. The Person of Jesus Christ
6. Personal experience

I am aware that these so-called facts may be explained differently by someone who does not believe as I do, but I simply ask you to look at these facts as I do and evaluate whether or not I have plausible evidence for the existence of God.

The Existence of the Material Universe

As a young boy, I often went to summer camp. Having been raised in the city, it was great to see some mountains, trees, and rivers. I was often impressed at night, while looking at the stars, at how great and vast our universe is. I felt great just staring into the stellar universe, admiring its beauty. As a boy, I began to conclude that someone bigger than you and I had to have made this universe. I also decided that if He made it, He had to be in existence *before* it was made. Simple logic!

Those two facts began to work on me. One, that whoever or whatever made this universe was in existence before it was made; and two, whoever or whatever caused it had to have enormous power and ability.

I later discovered that the Bible itself contains these basic arguments. Psalm 19:1 says, "The heavens declare the glory of God; And the firmament shows His handiwork." In the New Testament, we read: "For since the creation of the world His invisible attributes are *clearly seen,* being understood by the things that are made, even His eternal power and Godhead, so that they are without excuse" (Romans 1:20).

Could the universe come into existence out of nothing? Does no one plus nothing really equal something? I have read some of the world's scientific experts on the origin of the solar system and have been astonished at two things: Their disagreements with each other, and the assumptions they must "believe" in order to make their theories possible. Are the other explanations we have received more possible and probable than the existence of a Creator who brought it all into existence by His own power? Consider this statement by Professor Fred Hoyle, a renowned cosmologist from Cambridge University:

> I find myself forced to assume that the nature of the universe requires continuous creation—the perpetual bringing into being of new background material. . . . The most obvious question to ask about continuous creation is this: Where does the created material come from? It does not come from anywhere. Material appears—it is created. At one time the various atoms composing the material do not exist, and at a later time they do. This may seem a very strange idea, and I agree that it is, but in science it does not matter how strange an idea may seem so long as it works.
>
> *Harper's* magazine, Feb. 1951, p. 68*

---

* Quoted on p. 23 of the pamphlet, *The Origin of the Solar System,* by John C. Whitcomb (Philadelphia: Presbyterian and Reformed Publishing Co., 1964).

I find it much simpler to believe in the eternal existence and power of God!

The Order and Design of the Universe

From the telescopic world to the microscopic world, the facts reveal amazing order and mathematical design. The laws of gravity are difficult to comprehend. Why do the planets stay in orbit? Who can explain the incredible processes of nature, how things grow and why things die or decay? Yes, we can study and know the laws behind these questions, but how did it all happen? Why is it that way?

In the Bible's Book of Acts, two Christian leaders, Paul and Barnabas, confronted a pagan culture in the hills of central Turkey and said:

> Men, why are you doing these things? We also are men with the same nature as you, and preach to you that you should turn from these vain things to the living God, who made the heaven, the earth, the sea, and all things that are in them, who in bygone generations allowed all nations to walk in their own ways. Nevertheless, He did not leave Himself without witness, in that He did good, gave us rain from heaven and fruitful seasons, filling our hearts with food and gladness.
>
> Acts 14:15–17

Nature itself is a constant witness to the presence of a superior intelligence. It speaks of plan and design, not chance or chaos.

The Nature of Man

A class in basic anatomy really makes you think! Did man just evolve from lower life forms? Is the marvel of man's physical body the result of cosmic chance? I find that hard to believe! I do not want to just sweep all the theories of evolution under the rug or become like the proverbial ostrich with my head in the sand. But, on the other hand, I have some questions that are not answered by the theories of evolution, nor is the fact of my ability to reason about these questions easily explained apart from a Creator who has designed me like Himself—with a mind to think and an ability to reason beyond the immediate stimuli of my environment and personal needs.

In discussing my faith with a longtime friend from high school days, now teaching at one of the world's great universities in the area of physics and claiming to be an atheist, I was struck by the hopelessness of his personal views on man's existence. He is an evolutionist and believes that man is simply a higher form of animal. Realizing that his views offer little hope to the human race, he sees death as the ultimate enemy. He said, "When you're dead, you're dead!" He asked me how I believed that man was different from the animal world. Using an old argument with me— comparative anatomy—he said that any schoolchild could see that a monkey's development and bodily functions are similar to man's, and argued that this gave solid evidence for the probability that man evolved from the monkey. He added that it was only a question of time until that would be proven without a shadow of a doubt!

I said to him that with the same reasoning you could "prove" that a Cadillac evolved from a Volkswagen, since they both had steering wheels, four tires, and an engine that ran on gas! Does not it rather point to a designer who knew the needs of both?

The Bible teaches that man was created "in the image of God" (Genesis 1:26–27). Man's body was formed by God out of the elements of the soil—"the dust of the ground" (Genesis 2:7). Man's ability to function as a living organism was the result of the creative breath of God.

The simple beauty of the Bible's arguments about the nature of man is far more reasonable to me than the theory of evolution. The Book of Job speaks very clearly concerning the evidence of a Creator:

"But now ask the beasts, and they will teach you; And the

birds of the air, and they will tell you; Or speak to the earth, and it will teach you; And the fish of the sea will explain to you. Who among all these does not know that the hand of the LORD has done this, In whose hand is the life of every living thing, And the breath of all mankind?''

Job 12:7–10

In Psalms we read:

For You have formed my inward parts; You have covered me in my mother's womb. I will praise You, for I am fearfully and wonderfully made; Marvelous are Your works, And that my soul knows very well. My frame was not hidden from You, When I was made in secret, And skillfully wrought in the lowest parts of the earth. Your eyes saw my substance, being yet unformed. And in Your book they all were written, The days fashioned for me, When as yet there were none of them.

Psalm 139:13–16

When my wife delivered our first child, I was excited with that little baby! It was (and still is) a marvel to me, and that great event in our lives was another reminder of the existence of God. There simply had to be a Creator of enormous intelligence and power to design such creatures as we are. When I think of the amazing functions of the body—the eyes, ears, brain, nervous system, digestive system, and so on—I cannot help but believe that there is a God behind it all. I agree with the Apostle Paul's words in Acts 17:28: "For in Him [God] we live and move and have our being. . . ."

In 1 Corinthians 15:39, we read: "All flesh is not the same flesh, but there is one kind of flesh of men, another flesh of beasts, another of fish, and another of birds." That statement is clearly a contradiction to the theory of evolution. Man and woman are unique—not exalted or evolved animals!

Many people will label the arguments of those who believe that man's nature reveals the existence of God as "blind faith" and not based on facts. Bolton Davidheiser, says:

. . . most evolutionists have faith in the uniformity of
nature, which excludes miracles and other manifestations of
supernatural acts of God. They have faith that all life on earth
could have come about and did come about through the
interaction of blind forces acting upon the kinds of material
which were available before there was any life.*

It has to be *blind faith* that causes the evolutionist to begin with
nothing and produce something as marvelous and complex as the
nature of man. Surely it is more reasonable to believe that there
exists a Creator who made us in His own image.

Evolution must rule out the existence of God, especially a God
who created life in mature forms, capable of reproduction (cf.
Genesis 1). Evolution depends on a process which must move
from species to species in its development. We are told that this
process continues today, but that due to its slow development, it is
not observable.

The famous Mendel's Laws of genetics have shown the difficulties which the theories of evolution must face. They reveal that
descent from generation to generation is orderly rather than disor-
derly, that variation takes place within natural species as a result of
different combinations of materials already contained in the species, and that no new forms are ever created or introduced.

Moses, the great Jewish leader of over 3,000 years ago, claimed
that God spoke to him directly and said: "Who has made man's
mouth? Or who makes the mute, the deaf, the seeing, or the blind?
Have not I, the LORD?" (Exodus 4:11). The nature of man is a
tremendous evidence of the presence and existence of God!

The Reliability and Accuracy of the Bible

Out of all the religious literature of our world, one book stands
above all the rest in terms of authenticity, authority, reliability,

* *Evolution and Christian Faith* (Philadelphia: Presbyterian and Reformed
Publishing Co., 1969), pp. 150–151.

and historical accuracy. Before the printing press was ever developed, the Bible was by far the most copied book in all recorded history. The thousands of copies (done by hand) reveal an amazing dedication to its preservation and respect for its uniqueness.

I told a businessman at lunch one day that I had complete confidence in the reliability of the Bible. He blurted out, "That's stupid! It's full of contradictions and fairy tales!" I asked him to tell me at least one such contradiction or myth. He could not come up with any. The truth was that he, like so many people I have met, had never read the Bible!

If I did not believe in the existence of God, I would have a difficult time explaining the Bible itself. It was written by over forty different writers from different cultural backgrounds, writing over a period of 1,400 years. They speak about events and circumstances outside the realm of their immediate historical context. They all agree about God, His plan, and His ways. These writers speak of how God spoke to them directly, telling them what to write and directing their thoughts. They predict things about the future that we now know are fulfilled and completely accurate, although much of the Bible contains prophecies that are still unfulfilled.

The science of archaeology, which studies old civilizations, has continued to confirm the amazing accuracy of the Bible, even when the theories of man have contradicted it for many years. The Bible speaks of great civilizations in the past that we have only recently discovered did really exist. The digs of archaeologists have uncovered an enormous amount of evidence as to the reliability of the Bible concerning dates, names, places, events, and people of the past.

How do we explain all of this? Is it merely coincidence? How were these writers able to predict the rise and fall of nations before they ever came into existence? How can there be so much agreement, when the writers never met and lived hundreds of years apart?

The Person of Jesus Christ

How do we explain the Person of Jesus Christ without believing in the existence of God? He is without doubt the most outstanding and unique Person in the history of the world. There are over 300 prophecies about the Messiah in the Bible, written hundreds of years before Jesus Christ. He fulfilled all of them in one lifetime.

Who is Jesus Christ? The Bible claims He was born of a virgin—a biological miracle. He grew up in Nazareth, the son of a simple carpenter. At age twelve, His wisdom and teaching ability were noticed by the great theologians of Jerusalem. By the time He was thirty years of age, there were multitudes of people following Jesus, who claimed that He could heal the sick, the lame, the blind, and the deaf. He even raised people from the dead. Everywhere He went, He claimed to be able to forgive the sins of mankind. His miracles included authority over nature itself, as well as disease, suffering, and death.

The religious leaders of His day plotted to get rid of Him, and the Romans crucified Him, hoping to satisfy His enemies. According to the Bible, Jesus Christ arose from the dead and was seen by many people after His resurrection for forty days. He ascended into heaven and promised to return some day to this earth. He claimed to have the attributes and abilities of God Himself.

There was never any doubt among His contemporaries as to what He claimed. Some even wanted to stone Him on several occasions, accusing Him of blasphemy because He was making Himself equal with God.

How do we explain what history and the Bible claim about Jesus Christ? Was He God in human flesh—or simply paranoid with delusions of grandeur? Was He telling the truth—or was He a liar and imposter? Why did His disciples forsake Him at His crucifixion, but later die for Him after His resurrection? Did the writers of the New Testament really see Him and touch Him after His death and resurrection—or is that a big lie also?

The Bible tells us that Jesus Christ is "the image of the invisible God" (Colossians 1:15). It says that "in Him [Jesus] dwells all the fullness of the Godhead bodily" (Colossians 2:9), and "This is the true God and eternal life" (1 John 5:20).

Personal Experience

My experience is certainly not objective evidence concerning the existence of God. People can experience some incredible things which may or may not be a part of reality. The mind is capable of believing that something is real when it is not. What is real is what we *think* is real, but in terms of objective truth, it may or may not be real. I am capable of imagining a great deal, and so are you!

The experiences of those who believe in God are so varied, and at times strange, that one becomes cautious in using this argument to prove God's existence. But, in spite of the dangers involved, my experience is still something to be evaluated.

My parents became believers in God before I was born. I grew up in a home where it was assumed that God existed and that we were accountable to Him for our thoughts, words, and deeds. As a young boy, however, there were occasional doubts in my mind. The faith of my parents had to be "real" in *my* experience, or I knew that some day I would deny what they had taught me. I began to talk to God at an early age and seemed aware of my sin even before I went to school. Though I accepted Christianity as true when I was young, I had the kind of mind that demanded the facts. I began to question many things I was taught as a child, but I kept my doubts to myself, so others would not pressure me to believe what they did, or condemn me for questioning it.

The day that God's presence became real to me was the day that I placed my faith completely in the Bible. Everything I was asked to believe was to be found in the pages of the Bible. Either it was true or it wasn't. If it could not be trusted in some matters, how could I trust it at all?

You may think at this point that I made a mistake in putting such faith in the Bible, but the truth is that the more trust I had in the authority and reliability of the Bible, the more convinced I became of the Bible's teaching about the existence of God. Peace came into my life because of my faith in the Bible:

> By faith we understand that the worlds were framed by the word of God, so that the things which are seen were not made of things which are visible.
>
> Hebrews 11:3

> But without faith it is impossible to please Him, for he who comes to God must believe that He is, and that He is a rewarder of those who diligently seek Him.
>
> Hebrews 11:6

The reason why many people do not believe in the existence of God is that they do not put their faith in what the Bible says about God. My experience has continued to convince me that God really exists. I talk to Him every day, and He seems very close to me, as I share things with Him that I do not say to anyone else. I feel His love and presence, but am fully aware that this is rooted in my intellectual acceptance of the Bible's teaching about God. My feelings are not the proof of God's existence, but they exist (in my opinion) because He exists! He has honored my faith in the Bible by producing amazing results in my experience. I find that my experiences continue to teach me about the reality of God's presence, but it is the Bible itself that I trust. Faith in the Bible will bring the proper experiences. Do not trust your feelings—trust what the Bible says! Recognize that we are all subject to deception and misinterpretation in the realm of our feelings. We need to check out our feelings in the light of biblical truth. Believe it or not, your feelings are not always right!

Questions to Ponder

1. Why do people not believe in God's existence?
2. What experiences in your life have caused you to doubt that God really exists?

3. List some things about the universe that might point to God's existence rather than cosmic chance.

4. What facts about man suggest a Creator?

5. Why is the Bible so crucial to our belief in God's existence?

6. What do you really believe about Jesus Christ? Does your opinion check out with the facts?

2

How Does God Speak to Us?

If there is a God, it only makes sense to believe that He would try to communicate with the creatures He created. How does He do that? Is it possible for us to talk with Him or He with us?

As we all know, there are plenty of people around who claim that God talks to them. It gives them a feeling of superiority and dominance over others. Some of us may question them about this, only to discover that we become the "enemy of God" and our own spiritual relationship with God is denied by them! Does God really play favorites? Does He talk directly only to a select group (usually religious leaders)? Does He speak audibly to anyone today? Has He ever? Does He listen? I realize it is easier to ask the questions than answer them, but before I try to find the answers, I like to know what the questions are. If you feel as I do, you have lots of questions!

God Speaks Through What He Has Made

Assuming that you believe there is a God who made the universe and all that is in it, it is then natural to expect that God would speak to us through what He has made:

> The heavens declare the glory of God; And the firmament shows His handiwork. Day unto day utters speech, And night unto night reveals knowledge. There is no speech nor lan-

guage Where their voice is not heard. Their line has gone out
through all the earth, And their words to the end of the world.
Psalm 19:1–4

According to this Bible passage, God is constantly talking to us
through His material universe—and in all languages! We learn
about His "glory," His greatness. This can make you feel pretty
insignificant:

When I consider Your heavens, the work of Your fingers,
The moon and the stars, which You have ordained, What is
man that You are mindful of him, And the son of man that
You visit him?
Psalm 8:3–4

A few years ago, my wife and I were flying in an airplane over
the Swiss Alps. What a sight! The majestic beauty of those mountains is hard to describe to someone who has not seen them. They
reminded us of the greatness of God. While straining to look out
the airplane's window, I spilled my coffee and was quickly reminded of the frailty of man!

If you have ever visited the giant Sequoia trees in the mountains
east of Fresno, California, you have been impressed by their age
and size. What trees! They speak eloquently of the greatness of the
God who made them.

God's presence and greatness are revealed in the very processes
of nature. The Book of Job speaks of this:

Behold, God is great, and we do not know Him; Nor can the
number of His years be discovered. For He draws up drops of
water, Which distill as rain from the mist, Which the clouds
drop down and pour abundantly on man. Indeed, can anyone
understand the spreading of clouds, The thunder from His
canopy? Look, He scatters His light upon it, And covers the
depths of the sea. For by these He judges the peoples; He
gives food in abundance. He covers His hands with light-

ning, And commands it to strike. His thunder declares it, The cattle also, concerning the rising storm.

Job 36:26–33

When our oldest son was just a preschooler, he became frightened by one of those severe Midwest storms that sometimes hit central Ohio. When the thunder crashed, it seemed so close—and he wasn't the only one a little concerned during that particular storm! Much damage was done. When that first great clap of thunder hit, he asked, "Daddy, what's that?" I said, "That's God, letting us know how great He is!" He replied, "Could you ask Him not to talk so loud?"

Psalm 148:8 says: "Fire and hail, snow and clouds; Stormy wind, fulfilled His word." All nature speaks of the greatness and goodness of God. We would do well to look at the flowers more often!

God Speaks Through Supernatural Acts

The common processes of nature speak to us about God and His ways. But God has also spoken through some unusual acts by which He has intervened in the course of human history and let us all know that He exists, is powerful, and can change things whenever He wants.

In the Bible (Exodus 5–12), we have the story of the children of Israel in bondage to Egypt. Moses was chosen by God to go to Pharaoh, King of Egypt, and demand that he release the children of Israel from captivity and hard labor. Pharaoh, of course, was reluctant to believe that the God of Moses was powerful enough to pull it off or make him release them. The Bible tells us of ten plagues which God performed to impress Pharaoh of His power. God said to Moses:

> "And the Egyptians shall know that I am the Lord, when I stretch out My hand on Egypt and bring out the children of Israel from among them."

Exodus 7:5

It was also a part of God's strategy to speak to Israel by means of these signs and plagues. Moses told his people:

> "To you it was shown, that you might know that the LORD Himself is God; there is none other besides Him."
>
> Deuteronomy 4:35

The Bible also shows us that God was speaking to His people Israel when they were wandering in the wilderness for forty years. The Lord said to Moses:

> "How long will these people reject Me? And how long will they not believe Me, with all the signs which I have performed among them?"
>
> Numbers 14:11

These supernatural acts included bringing water out of a rock when they were thirsty, providing food—manna (a type of pastry) from heaven and quail from the sea—and guiding them with a cloud by day and a pillar of fire by night. God spoke through these miraculous signs, inviting His people to believe in Him.

The Book of Joshua tells us that God used miracles to speak to people at the time of Joshua's leadership as the children of Israel entered Canaan—their promised land:

> "For the LORD your God dried up the waters of the Jordan before you until you had crossed over, as the LORD your God did to the Red Sea, which He dried up before us until we had crossed over, that all the peoples of the earth may know the hand of the LORD, that it is mighty, that you may fear the LORD your God forever."
>
> Joshua 4:23–24

According to the New Testament, the supernatural works of God in the history of the Jewish people were written for our learning:

> Now all these things happened to them as examples, and they

were written for our admonition, on whom the ends of the ages have come.

1 Corinthians 10:11

The miracles of Jesus Himself were intended by God to speak to us:

> And truly Jesus did many other signs in the presence of His disciples, which are not written in this book; but these are written that you may believe that Jesus is the Christ, the Son of God, and that believing you may have life in His name.
> John 20:30–31

On one particular occasion, Jesus healed a man who was born blind. When His disciples asked about the cause of his blindness and suggested that it might be the result of sin, Jesus answered, "Neither this man nor his parents sinned, but that the works of God should be revealed in him" (John 9:3). The healing of this blind man was a message from God about His power.

A few years ago I was teaching a Bible study in the home of some friends whose daughter had become very ill with a high fever. Her temperature had been between 104° and 106° for about twenty-four hours, and since they could not get in touch with their doctor, they were becoming quite concerned. One of the members of that Bible study was a new Christian who, upon hearing of the little girl's fever, said, "Let's pray for her right now!" I said, "That's a great idea. Why don't you pray for her?" This was the first time this new Christian had ever prayed in public, and this is what she said: "God, if You can't heal this girl's fever right now, then I'm not going to believe in You anymore!" I was so embarrassed! I started to explain why we shouldn't *demand* that God heal people—because He is a sovereign God, and does what He pleases. To my surprise, the fever of that little girl immediately dropped to normal and never returned! I learned a lesson from one of God's miracles. They are intended to encourage us to believe in Him, and He can perform them any time He wants, even when the prayer asking Him to do it is not theologically correct!

Miracles can and do occur. They have happened before, and they still happen today. God is speaking through them to remind us of His power and greatness.

God Has Spoken Directly to Certain Individuals in the Past

Direct revelations of God to individuals in the past were the means by which God communicated His will and plan. The Bible records the following direct revelations in the Book of Genesis alone:

1. *To Adam and Eve*: Genesis 1:28–30
2. *To Adam*: Genesis 2:16–17; 3:9, 11, 17–19
3. *To Eve*: Genesis 3:13, 16
4. *To Cain*: Genesis 4:5–6, 9–12, 15
5. *To Noah*: Genesis 6:13–21; 7:1–4; 8:15–17
6. *To Noah and his sons*: Genesis 9:1–17
7. *To Abraham*: Genesis 12:1–3, 7; 13:14–17; 15:1, 4–5, 7, 9, 13–16, 18–21; 17:1–16, 19–22; 18:13–14, 17–21, 26, 28–33; 22:1–2, 16–18
8. *To Abimelech*: Genesis 20:3, 6–7
9. *To Rebekah*: Genesis 25:23
10. *To Isaac*: Genesis 26:2–5
11. *To Jacob*: Genesis 28:13–15; 32:26–29; 35:1, 10–13; 46:2–4
12. *To Laban*: Genesis 31:24, 29
13. *To Joseph*: Genesis 41:39

To this list, we could add the names of Moses, Aaron, Joshua, Balaam, Samuel, David, Solomon, Isaiah, Jeremiah, Ezekiel, Daniel, and many others. God spoke directly to them. Hundreds of times you will read the statement "thus says the Lord" or "the word of the Lord came unto me." In 2 Peter, we read:

> Knowing this first, that no prophecy of Scripture is of any private interpretation, for prophecy never came by the will of

man, but holy men of God spoke as they were moved by the
Holy Spirit.

2 Peter 1:20–21

God controlled what the prophets said in terms of what was
eventually written down. God guaranteed the reliability of what
was written by controlling the writers with His Holy Spirit.

At the time of Christ, God was still speaking directly, but main-
ly to His Son, Jesus Christ. On one occasion when God spoke from
heaven to His Son, the people who heard it misinterpreted it,
thinking it was thunder or that an angel had spoken to Him (John
12:28–29).

The Lord spoke directly to Saul of Tarsus on the road to
Damascus (Acts 9:4–6), and to Ananias who helped him (Acts
9:10–11, 15–16). He spoke to Peter (Acts 10:13–16), to Paul
(Acts 18:9–10; 23:11), and to John (Revelation).

Paul says that he received direct revelation from Jesus Christ
(Galatians 1:12) and adds that the information about the church
was revealed to God's "holy apostles and prophets" (Ephesians
3:2–5), who are called the "foundation" of the church (Ephesians
2:20).

It seems clear that God spoke directly in the past to a few
selected individuals. Most of these individuals were responsible
for what we now call the Bible. God spoke directly in the past to a
special group of people called prophets, but now has brought to a
close those days of speaking directly to men. His final message is
His Son, Jesus Christ (Hebrews 1:1–2). A clue as to the comple-
tion of God's direct messages to prophets is found in the last book
of the Bible, the Book of Revelation:

> For I testify to everyone who hears the words of the prophecy
> of this book: If anyone adds to these things, God will add to
> him the plagues that are written in this book; and if anyone
> takes away from the words of the book of this prophecy, God
> shall take away his part from the Book of Life, from the holy
> city, and from the things which are written in this book.

Revelation 22:18–19

God Speaks to Us Today Through the Bible

Though people claim that God talks to them directly, does the Bible teach that? People speak of "visions," "dreams," and "prophecies," and declare that God has given them direct revelation. The foundation of most cults and religions is the claim of direct revelation from God. But how do we know if they are telling the truth? Does God still speak audibly and directly to people apart from the Bible?

If God truly exists and has power as the Bible describes, then we would all agree that He can speak directly to people if He wants to do it. However, we all know how easy it is for people to believe that God talks to them directly, even if the facts do not prove that He did or would. Our problem is deciding whether or not this is the way God is doing it today.

In some respects, there would be advantages to God's speaking directly. It could save a lot of time and hard work. Assuming that God could speak in all the languages and dialects of the world, we would not have to go through all the trouble of learning to speak other languages and trying to translate the Bible into those languages.

The Bible was originally written in Hebrew, Aramaic, and Greek. Many people have a problem in hearing God speak to them through the Bible because of their language difficulties, their illiteracy, or the simple fact that they have never seen or read the Bible. If God does speak directly to people and He really cares about all language groups, then we would not need to spend so much time, effort, and money in trying to bring the Bible to them in their own language. Is God the God of the English-speaking world only? Does God not know how to speak the thousands of languages and dialects in the world?

I was watching a TV program where a man was claiming that God spoke directly to him. He gave some examples of things which God said to him would happen at certain times that have already proven incorrect. A well-known TV evangelist claims that God spoke to him directly and told him to build a certain facility, giving explicit instructions about how much money each person was to send in order to pay for it! Do you believe God did that? In my opinion, God is being blamed these days for a great deal of foolishness that is simply born in the mind of some clever and persuasive personalities!

What Guidelines Do We Have?

The Bible gives us some information as to how to evaluate people who claim that God is speaking directly to them.

1. If It Doesn't Happen, Then God Didn't Tell Them It Would!

> "And if you say in your heart, 'How shall we know the word which the LORD has not spoken?'—When a prophet speaks in the name of the LORD, if the thing does not happen or come to pass, that is the thing which the LORD has not spoken; the prophet has spoken it presumptuously; you shall not be afraid of him."
>
> Deuteronomy 18:21–22

Religious leaders often "predict" things to establish their authority or persuade people to do things they want them to do. If you want people to listen, just tell them that World War III will happen at a particular moment of history, and say that God told you it would. If you need money, just say that the Lord revealed to you how the money should be raised. If it does not happen, you can always blame the people for their lack of faith! Just tell people that God told you they would be healed of their cancer, and you will have their attention. If it fails to happen, you can always keep it quiet, or accuse them of not believing enough!

The tragedy is that many people are being hurt today by all these claims of direct revelation from God. If what they say does not happen, then God never told them it would!

2. If the Gospel That Is Preached Is Not the Gospel of Jesus Christ, Then God Did Not Speak to Them!

[Paul says:]

> I marvel that you are turning away so soon from Him who called you in the grace of Christ, to a different gospel, which is not another; but there are some who trouble you and want to pervert the gospel of Christ. But even if we, or an angel from Heaven, preach any other gospel to you than what we have preached to you, let him be accursed. As we have said before, so now I say again, if anyone preaches any other gospel to you than what you have received, let him be accursed. For do I now persuade men, or God? Or do I seek to please men? For if I still pleased men, I would not be a servant of Christ.
>
> Galatians 1:6–10

The gospel of Jesus Christ is clearly presented in the Bible. It includes the following, according to 1 Corinthians 15:1–11:

- Christ died for our sins, according to the Scriptures.
- He was buried.
- He rose again the third day, according to the Scriptures.
- He was seen by many people after He rose from the dead.
- You have to believe the gospel in order to be saved.

Other passages tell us that we are not saved by the works of the law or by our own efforts. Salvation is based on what Jesus Christ did, not what we do. Any gospel that emphasizes human merit, effort, or self-improvement is not the gospel of Christ! Any gospel that promotes health, wealth, or pleasure as the gospel of Christ is man-made, not from God. The issue is heaven or hell—where you will spend eternity. You may not believe what the Bible says, but do not be fooled by what some are saying is the true gospel.

We are warned in 2 John 7–11 about deceivers who do not teach the gospel of Jesus Christ. The Bible says that we are not to receive them or even encourage them in their work.

3. If What They Say Does Not Agree with the Bible, Then God Did Not Speak to Them!

The Prophet Isaiah says that God spoke directly to him with these words:

> And when they say to you, "Seek those who are mediums and wizards, who whisper and mutter," should not a people seek their God? Should they seek the dead on behalf of the living? To the law and to the testimony! If they do not speak according to this word, it is because there is no light in them.
> Isaiah 8:19–20

A man was in my office recently, informing me that God had spoken to him about a matter. The longer he talked, the more obvious it was that his view was a direct contradiction of the Bible's teaching. When I pointed out to him what the Bible says, he became indignant and accused me of unbelief and of suppressing the Spirit of God who was speaking to him. I told him that it was not God at all—and if someone or something did speak to him, it was probably satanic. He did not appreciate that and left my office abruptly.

The Book of Peter in the Bible was written to deal with false teachers who try to persuade people to follow *them* instead of the Bible. It warns: "By covetousness they will exploit you with deceptive words" (2 Peter 2:3), and "For when they speak great swelling words of emptiness, they allure through the lusts of the flesh" (verse 18). We also read:

> That you may be mindful of the words which were spoken before by the holy prophets, and of the commandment of us the apostles of the LORD and Savior.
> 2 Peter 3:2

The prophets and apostles who wrote the Bible are the ones to whom we should listen. This only emphasizes again the importance of the Bible as God's method of communication to us today.

4. If They Add Any Additional Truth to What the Bible Says, Then God Did Not Speak to Them!

There is no greater authority than the Bible! Even the church and its leaders have no authority over the Bible—they are submissive to the Bible itself. The Bible is a complete and final revelation from God. Revelation 22:18–19 tells us clearly that we cannot add to it or take away from it. Jude 3 tells us that the faith was "once for all delivered to the saints [all Christians]."

Paul speaks to Timothy of the uniqueness and adequacy of the written Bible for all of life and work:

> All Scripture [writing] is given by inspiration of God, and is profitable for doctrine, for reproof, for correction, for instruction in righteousness, that the man of God may be complete, thoroughly equipped for every good work.
>
> 2 Timothy 3:16–17

One man came up to me after I had finished speaking at a particular convention and proceeded to tell me the "new revelation" that God had given him. When he finished, I asked, "What verse?" He countered, "What do you mean by that?" I said, "Well, unless you show me where in the Bible it says what you just told me that God said to you, then I cannot accept or believe that God spoke to you." He blurted out, "This is additional to the Bible." I said, "Then God didn't tell you anything!" The "new revelation" dealt with his prediction that the world would blow up in 1975!

God Speaks to Us Through His Son, Jesus Christ!

Hebrews 1:2 says that God has "in these last days spoken to us by His Son." In John 14:8–9, Philip, one of the disciples of Jesus, said to Him: "Lord, show us the Father, and it is sufficient for us." Jesus answered, "Have I been with you so long, and yet you have not known Me, Philip? He who has seen Me has seen the Father; so how can you say, 'Show us the Father'?"

Jesus claims to be the revelation of the eternal God in human form. John 1:14 states that Jesus (the Word) "became flesh and dwelt among us, and we beheld His glory, the glory as of the only begotten of the Father, full of grace and truth." Verse 18 claims that Jesus revealed the invisible God to us.

Jesus Christ was born, lived, and died in a particular time and place in human history. So have others, but the Bible records facts about Him that are utterly amazing! It speaks of His miraculous birth—born of a virgin—no human father! It tells of His miracles, healing all kinds of diseases and performing supernatural acts that only the Creator could do. Jesus demonstrated (according to the Bible's account) control over the forces of nature. He claimed to forgive sin and to be able to raise the dead (which, according to the Bible, He did). He claimed to be able to give men eternal life if they would only believe in Him. Incredible claims! The Jewish leaders who lived in His time and heard His claims were convinced that Jesus was claiming to be God. They tried to stone Him for blasphemy, the final charge that led to His death. The Romans carried out the plans for His death by crucifying Him. History records these things—study them for yourself!

The most remarkable fact recorded in the Bible (and verified by other accounts, though not necessarily agreeing that it happened) is His own resurrection from the dead. The "empty tomb" stands as a silent, yet powerful witness to His resurrection. If there was any one fact of history that many tried to disprove more than all others, it was the resurrection of Jesus Christ from the dead. The Romans were terrified; the Jewish leaders did everything possible to stamp out what they believed was only a rumor. The fact is, no one could produce the dead bones of Jesus (which would have certainly dealt a heavy blow to Christianity in the beginning). Christianity spread like wildfire because of the resurrection of Jesus Christ from the dead! Many saw Him during the forty days

He was on the earth after His resurrection, before He ascended to heaven (according to the Bible, over 500 saw Him on one occasion).

You may not agree with what the Bible says about Jesus Christ, but make no mistake about what it is actually saying. The people who lived as contemporaries of Jesus Christ were not mistaken; they knew He was claiming to be God in human flesh. If Jesus is God, then obviously God has given us a revelation of Himself in human form. What better way to communicate with the human beings He Himself had created?

What are you going to do about Jesus Christ? Nothing? Remain neutral? Impossible! You are either going to reject Him and His claims (no matter how often you commend Him for being a good person or teacher), or you are going to fall down at His feet and proclaim Him as your Lord and Saviour. Neutral you cannot be! He is either a severe paranoid with unbelievable delusions of grandeur; a liar and hypocrite of incredible proportions; a victim of what others were saying about Him (all of whom forsook Him at the cross); well-meaning, but unable to face the truth; or He is who He claimed to be—Lord of the universe, God in human flesh, our only Saviour from sin. Make your choice!

If I wanted to communicate with some ants crawling on the ground, how would I do it most effectively? If possible, the most logical way would be to become an ant. God became man to communicate with us in the Person of Jesus Christ.

Questions to Ponder

1. What does God say to us through the material universe?
2. What do miracles tell us? Can they happen today?
3. Why did God speak directly to people in the past?
4. How do we know whether God has spoken directly to someone today?
5. Why is the Bible so important in hearing what God has to say?
6. Who is Jesus Christ? Do you believe what the Bible says about Him?

3

Is God a Real Person?

Depending upon some*thing* rather than a special some*one* does not bring real security. If God is nothing more than a force, idea, or principle, there will be little impact upon us in terms of a personal relationship or involvement. The God who can help us the most is a personal God: One who knows how we feel and think, and who knows our needs.

To many people, God is a security blanket. He is no more personal to them than a chair or table. They hope He exists, but they have little knowledge of Him and no personal contact with Him. To such people, God is an "it" rather than "He." They regard God as the "force" which they hope will "be with them."

Is God like we are? Does He have a personality as we do? Does He have emotions as we have? Can we relate to Him personally as we do our friends? Do we share common characteristics? Does He have a body like ours? Is He physical at all? Can we see Him? Can we experience Him through the five senses?

I asked a group of third-graders what they thought God was like, and one boy said, "I hope He's like my dad." When I asked him why, he replied, "Because my dad really likes me!"

The importance of discovering that God is a real Person cannot be emphasized enough to a generation that views God from a distance and spends little time learning about Him. I believe that He is as real and personal as any one of us.

What Is a Person?

It is very difficult to establish the personality of God without first determining what makes a person a person. One of the older viewpoints of personality is that it consists of three parts: Mind, emotions, and will. But personality is more than that, since, to a certain degree, all animals reflect intelligence, feelings, and will. The Bible teaches that animals were created by God (Genesis 1:20–25), but they are never said to be "in the image of God." Only man is made in God's own "image" and after His "likeness" (Genesis 1:26–27).

We have a dog named Angie. She is a real lover and seems like a member of the family. At times, she seems almost human. She communicates with us in various ways and gets very excited about seeing us when we come home from work each day. She obeys our commands and seems to sense our moods and respond accordingly. Although she reflects certain characteristics of personality, Angie is just a dog. Her level of intelligence and her ability to communicate are extremely limited. We realize that she can neither reason as we do nor plan for the future. She simply responds to the direct stimuli of her physical needs or the demands of her environment. She can be trained and tamed, but rational thought is impossible for her.

A person is more than an animal, although an animal has a physical body, as do we. But when man was made "in the image of God," that did not refer to a physical body, since the Bible teaches that God did not have a physical body when man was created. Although many physical characteristics are attributed to God (such as "the hand of the Lord" or "the eye of the Lord"), these are simply descriptions of the attributes of God in terms that we can easily understand and with which we can readily identify.

Jesus says, "God is Spirit" (John 4:24). That means that His basic nature is spiritual rather than physical. Man has a spirit, soul, and body (1 Thessalonians 5:23). Physical death occurs when the body is separated from the spirit: "The body without the spirit is dead" (James 2:26). The soul or personality of man never dies. It is eternal, although the body will decay in the dust of the ground when physical death occurs.

The ways in which God is the same as man deal with personality only. Man is limited in function, ability, understanding, potential, and so on, whereas God's personality is unlimited. Man's personality has been deeply affected by sin, whereas God's has not.

The Apostle Paul dealt with this problem in his message to the Epicurean and Stoic philosophers of the city of Athens. This is recorded in Acts 17:24–29 (see *Introduction*). God's greatness is clearly established in this message. Paul also clearly teaches that man is "His offspring." Man is created by God in God's own image!

A real person exists *because* God exists. Personality exists because God is a Person. God did not make animals in His own image, and man's *physical* body is not in God's image (it comes from the dust of the ground from which God made it). Man's body is not the same as his soul and his spirit. God *is* Spirit, but man *has* a spirit. Man is not spirit alone, but spirit, soul, and body.

What is a person? Let's begin by stating what it is not: A person is not merely a body. A person is not an animal.

Basic Characteristics of Personality

While some of these can be seen in limited ways in the animal world, it is the combination of these characteristics that makes personality what it is and the unique possession of human beings.

1 *Life:* It should be obvious that personality is a part of what lives, not what is dead. A dead body has no personality. It is said of God the Son: "In Him was life, and the life was the light of men" (John 1:4). God breathed into man's nostrils the breath of life (Genesis 2:7), and man became a living soul. John 5:26 says: "For as the Father has life in Himself, so He has granted the Son to have life in Himself." We also are told: "Now to the King eternal, immortal, invisible, to God who alone is wise, be honor and glory forever and ever. Amen" (1 Timothy 1:17). God is *immortal* and *eternal*. We live because God lives.

Deuteronomy 5:26 connects the "living God" with the ability to speak: "For who is there of all flesh who has heard the voice of the living God speaking from the midst of the fire, as we have, and lived?"

In 1 Timothy 4:10, the "living God" is connected with salvation: "For to this end we both labor and suffer reproach, because we trust in the living God, who is the Savior of all men, especially of those who believe." Because He lives, God is able to do things which the non-living cannot do.

> For we know Him who said, "Vengeance is Mine; I will repay, says the LORD." And again, "The LORD will judge His people." It is a fearful thing to fall into the hands of the living God.
>
> Hebrews 10:30–31

Because He lives, He can and will judge. We are told: ". . . For He is the living God, And steadfast forever; His kingdom is the one which shall not be destroyed, And His dominion shall endure to the end. He delivers and rescues, And He works signs and wonders In heaven and on earth, Who has delivered Daniel from the power of the lions" (Daniel 6:26–27). It is the God who lives who delivers His people. He is a real Person because He lives! The non-living is the non-personal. What comfort this should be to our hearts!

There is a popular Christian song written by Bill Gaither that says:

> "Because He lives, I can face tomorrow;
> Because He lives, all fear is gone;
> Because I know He holds the future
> And life is worth the living just because He lives!"*

In Matthew 22:23–32, a group of religious teachers approach

---

* "Because He Lives," by William J. and Gloria Gaither. Copyright © 1971 by William J. Gaither. Used by permission.

Jesus Christ with a hypothetical problem concerning the resurrection of the dead (which they do not believe). They say that a man died, leaving a wife without any children. The man had seven brothers who all married their brother's wife, and each one died before having any children. They then ask Jesus, "Therefore, in the resurrection, whose wife of the seven will she be? For they all had her." Jesus tells them that there are no marriage relationships in heaven, and knowing that they did not believe in the resurrection of the dead, He poses a problem for them to solve. He quotes Exodus 3:6, in which God said to Moses, "I am the God of your father—the God of Abraham, the God of Isaac, and the God of Jacob" (all of whom had died many years previous to this). Jesus then says, "God is not the God of the dead, but of the living." No Jew would deny that God is the God of Abraham, Isaac, and Jacob. But it is obvious that they were still alive at the time of Moses, even though it was over 600 years after their death!

The first and primary mark of personality is life. God is a living Person, and so are we. Several years ago my wife and I were in the Soviet Union. While in the city of Moscow, our Russian guide was quite insistent that we stand in line with thousands of Russians who were waiting to visit the tomb of Nicolai Lenin, the founder of communism and leader of the Bolshevik revolution in 1917. We told our guide that we didn't care to see the tomb. She asked why. I replied, "because he is dead." She inquired why that was such a problem. I told her that I believed in the living God and in the resurrection of the dead. We were interested in life, not death. That conversation led to three days of continual discussion (and some argument) about God and the fact that He is a Person and living. Before we left Moscow, she also became a believer in the living, personal God, about whom she had never heard before our conversation that day in Red Square.

2. *Self-consciousness:* Some have called this the fundamental mark of personality. The fact that I know that I exist, that I am aware of my existence and personality, is evidence of my personhood. One of the great statements of the Bible about the self-consciousness of God Himself is contained in His words to Moses: "I AM WHO I AM" (Exodus 3:14).

Paul tells us in 1 Corinthians 2:11: "For what man knows the things of a man except the spirit of the man which is in him? Even so no one knows the things of God except the Spirit of God." No one knows my thoughts (except God), and no man knows the thoughts of God—but God does. God is completely and thoroughly self-conscious, whereas man's self-consciousness is incomplete. That point is clearly brought out in this biblical passage:

> Search me, O God, and know my heart; Try me, and know my anxieties; And see if there is any wicked way in me, And lead me in the way everlasting.
>
> Psalm 139:23–24

Although man does have self-consciousness, he does not know himself as God knows him:

> "The heart is deceitful above all things, And desperately wicked; Who can know it? I, the Lord, search the heart, I test the mind, Even to give every man according to his ways, And according to the fruit of his doings."
>
> Jeremiah 17:9–10

We do not know ourselves as God knows us, but we do have a great deal of self-conciousness.

Another example of self-consciousness is this statement in John 6:6: "But this He [Jesus] said to test him, for He Himself knew what He would do." Jesus was obviously self-conscious in this situation.

Two people can look alike physically. We call them twins, and when there is a remarkable resemblance, we call them *identical* twins. But twins can have very different personalities, and each of them is aware of his or her individuality. Each is self-conscious, and that awareness distinguishes him or her from the twin who physically looks the same. In one sense, they are the same; but in the other sense, they are different from each other.

Our self-consciousness makes each of us unique and special to God. This characteristic of God's personality brings much comfort to us, as it elevates us above the animal world and makes us much more than robots fashioned just like everyone else. We are aware of our unique existence, conscious that we are unlike those around us, although we are similar in so many ways. We are special to God, made in His own image!

3. *Freedom:* Animals are not free. They cannot arise above their circumstances. Man can, although man is not completely free—as God is. Nothing outside of Himself controls the actions and decisions of God. Man is free to the degree that God allows him to operate. Freedom does not mean that we can do anything we want to do, although some people teach that this is a possibility for man. Even God is not free in this sense, since God is limited by Himself. His own character and attributes control His actions and decisions. When we speak of freedom, we are speaking of the ability to determine our actions and decisions.

". . . He does according to His will in the army of heaven And among the inhabitants of the earth. No one can restrain His hand Or say to Him, 'What have You done?' " (Daniel 4:35). That's freedom! That's a mark of personality. Job 23:13 adds: "But He is unique, and who can make Him change? And whatever His soul desires, that He does." Nothing outside of Himself controls God's acts and purposes—". . . according to the purpose of Him who works all things according to the counsel of His will" (Ephesians 1:11). He makes the decisions in and of Himself. He is totally free in that sense: "But our God is in heaven; He does whatever He pleases" (Psalm 115:3), and "Whatever the Lord pleases, He does. . . ." (Psalm 135:6).

Several years ago, during the days of student unrest and revolution, I was speaking about the presence and existence of God from the steps of Sproul Hall at the University of California, Berkeley. One of the students called out and said, "Can God make a rock that He cannot move?" I answered, "Yes and no. He can make a rock, but He will not make one He cannot move. He does nothing to violate His character. He is limited by who He is, but absolutely free to do what He wants to do. He obviously does not want to do it!''

What about man? Is man free? Yes and no. Man is free to act within the boundaries which God has determined and set. If man chooses to sin (which, in a sense, he is free to do), he loses a measure of his freedom by experiencing the consequences of his act. His freedom produces a loss of freedom. Man is free to make decisions, but factors outside of himself often control his freedom. Not so with God.

I remember well the high school student who told me he was free to make his own decisions. He wanted freedom from his parents and all who were in authority over him. He started into drugs, all in the name of freedom. His habit required more money, and he started stealing. Eventually he was arrested and put in prison. When I visited him in prison, I asked, ''Do you still want your freedom?'' He said, ''No!'' His so-called freedom had now made him a slave, a captive of his own selfish and rebellious desires. Freedom to him now meant that he wanted to get out of prison, where his original idea of freedom had placed him.

Some people teach that man is not free at all. A certain fatalism characterizes their view and encourages a passive attitude toward life, assuming that everything is outside of their ability to act and affect changes. That brings no comfort at all. Our comfort resides in the fact that being made in God's image, we are like Him in personality. Because He is free, we also have a measure of freedom to act, think, and speak. It is encouraging to know that I am free (within certain limitations) to live for the glory of God, and not forced to act with mindlessness and meaninglessness in my life.

4. *Purpose:* Animals have no purpose. They simply react to the stimuli of their physical needs or the environment. God has purpose. Ephesians 3:11 speaks of His ''eternal purpose.'' His purpose includes everything: ''For of Him [source] and through Him [channel] and to Him [goal] are all things, to whom be glory forever. Amen'' (Romans 11:36).

The purpose or plan of God is constantly referred to in the Bible. Isaiah 23:9 says, ''The LORD of hosts has purposed it.'' In Isaiah

14:26–27, we read: "This is the purpose that is purposed against the whole earth, And this is the hand that is stretched out over all the nations. For the LORD of hosts has purposed, And who will annul it?" Isaiah 43:13 makes this claim: "Indeed before the day was, I am He; And there is no one who can deliver out of My hand; I work, and who will reverse it?" That is what I call a plan! Nothing can change it!

We have purpose just as God does, but our purpose is limited by *His* purpose and plan. His purpose includes everything; ours does not. When we react to some future goal, which actually exists only in our minds, we are said to have purpose. We can react to the stimuli of future goals which have no real existence outside of our own minds. This is what we mean by purpose, and it is a mark of personality. Animals do not possess it. The difference between our purpose and God's purpose is that our purpose does not always turn out as we planned. His purpose is always fulfilled! His personality means that there is purpose to all that is happening in our lives: "And we know that all things work together for good to those who love God, to those who are the called according to His purpose" (Romans 8:28).

A severely handicapped friend has had much frustration over the matter of purpose. What purpose did God have in allowing her disability? She often asked about the meaning of her life, being paralyzed and confined to a wheelchair. Because life seemed so hopeless to her and without any design or plan, telling her about God and His plan for our lives has not been easy. At times, what I had to say seemed so academic and indifferent to her need. However, it was the knowledge of the Bible about the plan and purpose of God that brought relief and joy to her. My friend began to understand how the purpose of God's personality was also a part of her. She began to grasp the importance of purpose in her own life and found tremendous happiness in helping other handicapped people. She "purposed" to help others and "planned" what she could and would do. In all of this, she discovered what being a person is all about, in spite of a physical body that did not function well.

My legs are a part of me, but they are not *me*. My hand does what I command it to do, but without its use, I am still who I am. My personality is something more than my physical body, although the two must dwell together in order for physical life to exist.

5. *Intelligence:* A certain level of intelligence exists in the animal world. They can learn to do things through training. We had to train our dog to go outside through a small door that I made in our back door. Our dog is intelligent enough to know by the sound of our voices when we are upset with her. But the intelligence of animals is limited by factors (physical needs, environment, punishment, reward, and so on) which do not limit man. There are three phases to the intelligence of man which reveal his superiority over the animal world.

- *Knowledge*—the perception of facts as they are. God is perfect in this regard. Man does not always perceive the facts correctly.
- *Understanding*—the insight into the meaning of these facts. Man has the ability to understand; animals do not. God has perfect understanding of all things.
- *Wisdom*—the ability to relate facts to each other and use for good ends. Man has the ability to apply what he knows. God's wisdom is perfect and good. Animals have no such ability.

"For the LORD is the God of knowledge," says 1 Samuel 2:3. His intelligence has resulted in creative acts. Proverbs 3:19–20 states: "The Lord by wisdom founded the earth; By understanding He established the heavens; By his knowledge the depths were broken up, And clouds drop down the dew." Concerning the personal Messiah who will come, Isaiah 11:2 says, "The Spirit of the Lord shall rest upon Him, The Spirit of wisdom and understanding, The Spirit of counsel and might, The Spirit of knowledge and of the fear of the LORD."

While intelligence is a mark of personality, God's level of intelligence also separates Him from man. God is omniscient (all-knowing) and man is not. But the fact that man has intelligence—a mind to think, reason, and plan—results from God's placing within man His own image. We think, because God thinks. We understand, because God understands. He is a personal God, because He has intelligence—and we are persons, because we are made in His image.

In the Book of Job is an interesting commentary on the subject of knowledge and understanding:

> "From where then does wisdom come? And where is the place of understanding? It is hidden from the eyes of all living, And concealed from the birds of the air. Destruction and Death say, 'We have heard a report about it with our ears!' God understands its way, And He knows its place. For He looks to the ends of the earth, And sees under the whole heavens, To establish a weight for the wind, And mete out the waters by measure. When He made a law for the rain, And a path for the thunderbolt, Then He saw wisdom and declared it; He prepared it, indeed, He searched it out. And to man He said, 'Behold, the fear of the Lord, that is wisdom, And to depart from evil is understanding.' "
>
> Job 28:20–28

Though man knows, he cannot know where the ability to know comes from, unless He looks to God for that knowledge. For God is the source of intelligence, because God is a Person. His ability to know, reason, and understand was given to man when man was created in His own image.

There is tremendous comfort in knowing that God is a real Person with great intelligence and understanding. I do not know why some events happen as they do, nor do I understand many things. But I know God does, and I relax in that truth. It gives me great comfort to know that He knows and understands. My children have had to learn that same truth in their dependence upon me and the decisions that I must make in their behalf, as a father.

6. *Emotion:* God is emotional and has feeling just as much as we do (in fact, more!). Personality requires emotional response. Animals display emotions. They get angry and they can be sad, but the emotional response of animals in no way compares with that of man. It is extremely confined and limited by physical need and environment. Animals respond only to the stimuli in their immediate situation. Man can become emotional about the past or the future and can have feelings without facts. People can create emotion within the framework of their own mind. Feelings of hate and bitterness can exist when no real cause for them exists.

One woman I know is a sad example of how emotions can dominate people's lives, even when there is no apparent reason for them. She imagines that people do not like her, although she has no evidence that this is their actual response. When she goes to the store for groceries, she believes others are talking about her and even plotting to kill her. She lives in constant fear and has withdrawn herself completely from social contact with other people. The blinds in her home are always closed, although she peeks out the window of her home from time to time to see if anyone is outside, planning how to attack her. Fortunately, she finally went for professional counseling and help and is learning to overcome her fears. Her emotions have controlled her, yet were created within her own mind. Though sad, it is another remarkable fact about personality. We have emotions that are totally unrelated to our environment or our actual circumstances.

Emotions are displayed through the physical body, but not necessarily out of necessity. Some people feel sorrow when there are no tears, and no one can discern it by physical characteristics. Some people love when the physical actions of the body do not show it. We are often unaware of the feelings of others, but when they are outwardly displayed, we become more aware. However, it is possible for the human personality outwardly to display emotion that is not inwardly felt. We can be deceived by outward emotions. Hebrews 12:17 says of Esau that "he found no place for repentance, though he sought it diligently with tears." In 2 Corinthians 7:9, Paul says: "Now I rejoice, not that you were made sorry, but that your sorrow led to repentance."

Perhaps no other mark of personality is as important to us as that of emotional response. We live in an age when emotions dominate. What feels good is what we determine to be right and valid.

The word *self* has become a common word in our literature and conversations. We emphasize our needs and desires and speak often about whether anyone really cares about us. "Being a real person" has come to be identified with emotional response. Personality is certainly characterized by emotion and feeling, but it is only a part of what personality is.

God Is Emotional!

God is emotional, just as we are. We sense that He is personal in a greater way when we know that He feels as we do—and need to do. Consider the following emotions that God has.

Love: "Yes, I have loved you with an everlasting love . . ." (Jeremiah 31:3).

"For God so loved the world. . . ." (John 3:16).

These words and countless similar verses in the Bible are most reassuring to believers that God is personal and deeply identifies with them.

Though our ability to love is not always what we want it to be, its very presence is one of the great marks of personality. It is possible to feel love for others without ever touching them or talking to them. It is also possible to touch someone with physical affection and not feel love. Sometimes we feel physical and sexual desire by looking or touching, yet there is absolutely no regard for how the other person feels. Sexual acts are often unloving and most unsatisfactory, because they become merely animal response rather than a loving act by a personality within a physical body. Bodies function, but persons love.

In talking with a teenage girl who had lost her sense of self-worth and respect through many sexual encounters, I inquired about what she really wanted in life. Without hesitation, she said, "Someone to really love me!" She had heard boys telling her that they loved her, only to take advantage of her sexually. She had now become very aware of the difference between outward appearance and inward feelings or personality.

Just as we can feel and experience love for someone we cannot touch or talk to, so we can experience God's love for us. He is a real Person and the Bible teaches much about His wonderful, unconditional love.

In Ephesians 2:4, we learn that God is merciful toward us "because of His great love with which He loved us." He knows what we are like, and yet He still loves us!

Husbands are told to love their wives as Jesus Christ "loved the church and gave Himself for it" (Ephesians 5:25). The personal, warm, encouraging, supportive love of God was demonstrated by the act of sending His Son to die on a cross for our sins:

> In this the love of God was manifested toward us, that God has sent His only begotten Son into the world, that we might live through Him. In this is love, not that we loved God, but that He loved us and sent His Son to be the propitiation for our sins. Beloved, if God so loved us, we also ought to love one another.
>
> 1 John 4:9–11

Hate: In Psalm 5:5, we read: "You hate all workers of iniquity." Deuteronomy 16:22 says, "You shall not set up a sacred pillar, which the LORD your God hates." Proverbs 6:16 adds: "These six things the Lord hates, Yes, seven are an abomination to Him." In Isaiah 1:14, the Lord says, "Your New Moons and your appointed feasts, My soul hates. . . ."

There are many people who do not like to believe that God hates. They picture Him as the One who loves without any possibility of hatred. But if God did not hate as well as love, He would be something less than a total personality. A real person both loves and hates.

Hate is one emotion that troubles us all. I hate myself sometimes for the stupid things I do. I also hate weeds! I hate the things people do to hurt other people. I hate injustice, I hate some problems that seem to kill my most productive times, and I often hate the telephone—just for ringing again!

Last week I was hating the times in which someone or something interrupted my ability to study and have time to myself. It was really getting to me. I wanted to throw or break something, but I was concerned that it be something of little value—and nothing seemed handy. I started to laugh. How silly for me to be so upset! And yet, I was manifesting that I am a real person, because I have these feelings. God has them too, but His hatred is always justified and rooted in His knowledge of all things. Somehow, I felt closer to God that day, even through my hate!

Anger: Wrath or anger is a common emotion of God. The Bible speaks often of God's angry wrath. Romans 1:18 says that "the wrath of God is revealed from heaven against all ungodliness and unrighteousness of men, who suppress the truth in unrighteousness." Revelation 14:10 speaks of the "wrath of God, which is poured out full strength into the cup of His indignation." The seven last plagues upon the world are described in Revelation 15:7 as "full of the wrath of God." John 3:36 says, "He who believes in the Son has everlasting life; and he who does not believe the Son shall not see life, but the wrath of God abides on him." Hell itself is an expression of the wrath of God against unbelief and sin.

It is right to be angry, but we are told to "be angry, and do not sin" (Ephesians 4:26). There is always a danger of sinning when you are angry. But anger, in and of itself, is not sinful. We ought to be angry at sin and evil, although we ought to love the sinner. Anger is an emotion that a real personality will express.

Hate and anger are closely related. Hate means that I don't like something or someone, and anger is the emotional result. My anger is sometimes displayed when the matter at hand seems so very insignificant. I can get angry at the failures of others, even when there is no reason why they should have acted in my behalf. Dogs can be trained or stimulated to anger, but sitting by themselves without such outside influence, they will never be angry. We have the ability as persons to become angry without experiencing any justifiable reason for our reaction.

I was amused at our dog a few weeks ago. She normally is very docile and loves to lie around all day in the warm sun. But she does get angry at birds that invade her territory. While watching her through the window, I noticed that she got real upset at this one bird in our yard and took off running after that bird. She was so excited that she slipped on the wet cement and fell into our pool. Her anger was immediately transformed into cries for help. I pulled her out, and she played the role of a hurt puppy who needed lots of love, which, of course, she got—I'm a soft touch!

God gets angry, and He never does wrong. His anger is one more piece of evidence that He is a real person. I can relate to Him because I know what anger is like. The more I learn about God and His anger, the better able am I to understand myself and learn to control my emotional outbursts.

Sorrow: In Isaiah 53:3, the Messiah is called "a Man of sorrows and acquainted with grief," and 2 Corinthians 7:10 speaks of sorrow that is "godly." In Jeremiah 8:18, the prophet says, "I would comfort myself in sorrow; My heart is faint in me." In Genesis 6:6, we read: "And the LORD was sorry that He had made man on the earth, and He was grieved in His heart."

It is a mark of personality that we have sorrow and grief—and a comfort to know that God feels sorrow as well. He is a real Person. He understands our tears and feels as we do about the heartaches in life. Knowing that God feels sorrow is one of the great encouragements to me. It helps me relate to Him emotionally.

My sense of grief was expanded a few years ago when I experienced some deep disappointments and hurts from people who I thought were my friends. I was astonished at their lack of concern and compassion for me in that particular situation. I remember feeling the hurt so deeply that I thought my insides were going to explode! I wanted someone with whom I could share my grief. I remember the comfort I received from a friend who had suffered greatly in much the same way as I had. He identified with me in so many ways that I knew he had experienced such hurt also, and somehow it helped to know that he understood what I was going through. That caused me to understand my personal relationship with God in a deeper way. God knows and feels sorrow, just as I do. He is a real Person who can identify with what I am experiencing.

We have a Friend who can "sympathize" with us (Hebrews

4:15). In the Book of Psalms, we read: "Cast your burden on the Lord, and He will sustain you. . .." (55:22), and "Trust in Him at all times, you people; Pour out your heart before Him; God is a refuge for us" (62:8). Because God is a personal God, He can comfort us in our sorrow and grief, for He Himself is acquainted with all that we feel.

Compassion: Animals do not care, but God cares, and people care. Compassion is a characteristic of personality that makes it unique: "As a father pities his children, so the LORD pities those who fear Him" (Psalm 103:13). The Bible speaks often of the mercies, graciousness, and compassion of our God. How wonderful to know! How could we doubt that He is a real Person after learning of His great compassion? Lamentations 3:22 reminds us: "Through the LORD's mercies we are not consumed, because His compassions fail not."

Most of us feel compassion at times, especially when we are confronted with human need. I felt compassion for a little five-year-old girl who was crying in the middle of a giant shopping mall because she was lost and could not find her parents. It was a joy to help her and see how her fears turned to happiness when she saw her parents again. I also felt compassion for a man without legs who was begging on the street for someone to help him get into his wheelchair. It was a pleasure to help him.

When my wife and I were in Cairo, Egypt, several years ago, we saw so much poverty in certain sections of that city that we felt compassion and pity and wished we could do something for these people. We have often felt that way in many parts of the world.

Compassion is caring about people in need, and God has it in abundance, because He is a real Person. His Son, Jesus, manifested it on so many occasions. Matthew 9:36 says, "But when He saw the multitudes, He was moved with compassion for them, because they were weary and scattered, like sheep having no shepherd." In Matthew 15:32, Jesus says, "I have compassion on the multitude, because they have now continued with Me three days and have nothing to eat. And I do not want to send them away hungry, lest they faint in the way."

One of the most beautiful stories about the compassion of God is found in the Gospel of Luke, chapter 15: The story of the Prodigal Son. After leaving his father's home, spending all his fortune, and winding up in a pigpen, the son began to realize what he had done and decided to return to his father. The Bible says in Luke 15:20, ". . . when he was still a great way off, his father saw him and had compassion, and ran and fell on his neck and kissed him." That's true compassion! God is a Person and, because of that, has great compassion for all of our needs.

Jealousy: The strong emotion of jealousy can be either good or bad. God is described as a "jealous God" in Deuteronomy 5:9. He does not want His people worshiping any false gods and declares that His people must worship only Him. We also read this in Exodus 20:5: "I, the Lord your God, am a jealous God." Exodus 34:14 goes so far to say, ". . . for the Lord, whose name is Jealous, is a jealous God." The Lord is jealous for His land and for Jerusalem and Zion (Joel 2:18; Zechariah 1:14, 8:2).

Proverbs 6:34 speaks of how "jealousy is a husband's fury," and Song of Solomon 8:6 says that "jealousy [is] as cruel as the grave."

Do you remember how jealous you felt when the person you loved was with someone else? Jealousy is a powerful emotion. Sometimes we are jealous of the benefits others have or the achievements they accomplish. That is the dark side of jealousy. When we are jealous over our wives and children, seeking to protect them and provide for them, that is the good side. Jealousy is good when the motive and result are right. The lack of jealousy in a husband's heart when his wife is being exploited by other men is simply evidence of a dying love for her. Love will often result in the emotion of jealousy.

Because God feels jealousy, I have one more evidence that He is a real Person with whom I can easily identify.

Joy: What a wonderful emotion joy is! Personality is also characterized by feelings of joy and happiness. God feels joy as surely as we do. Isaiah 62:5 says, "So shall your God rejoice over you." In Psalm 16:11, David wrote: "In Your presence is fullness of joy; At Your right hand are pleasures forevermore." Nehemiah 8:10

says that "the joy of the LORD is your strength." Zephaniah 3:17 tells us that "He will rejoice over you with gladness . . . with singing." Our God is emotional in His response! He is a real Person.

We feel joy when a new baby is born into our family. We feel joy when our children bring home a report card for which they and we parents are proud. Joy fills us when our children make the team or are chosen for special awards or honors. We have joy when our children get married and when the job we wanted becomes ours. News of a pay increase or special gifts that were unexpected can bring us joy. Joy is a common emotion to persons. And God has it also!

When we learned that the interest rate on a first trust deed for our new home was going to be assumable at a much lower rate than we had anticipated, there was great joy in our hearts! Knowing that God is a God of joy, I felt close to Him then and believed that He had joy with us over that matter.

Jesus tells us in Luke 15:10 that "there is joy in the presence of the angels of God over one sinner who repents." Heaven is a place of joy, and God is a Person with great joy for His people!

A Personal Relationship Is Possible!

We have shared six basic characteristics of personality that reveal God to be a real Person. He is approachable and knowable because of it. He possesses life, self-consciousness, freedom, purpose, intelligence, and emotion. So do we. Although we are limited in the expression and depth of these characteristics, we have them because we were made "in the image of God." We have personalities because God does.

The Bible does not speak of God in neuter terms. He is not an "it." Personal pronouns are used of Him, and He possesses all the marks of personality. He is personal in every way, and that means that a personal relationship with Him is possible for every one of us. Do *you* have this personal relationship with God?

Abraham was called "the friend of God" (James 2:23) because

he put his complete trust in God. Israel's King David was referred to as "a man after God's own heart." In 2 Corinthians 6:18, we are told that God has said: "I will be a Father to you, and you shall be My sons and daughters." This personal relationship is like a family. God becomes our Father, and we His children.

John 1:12 says, "As many as received Him [Jesus], to them He gave the right to become children of God, even to those who believe in His name." And 1 John 3:1 declares, "Behold what manner of love the Father has bestowed on us, that we should be called children of God!" Our personal relationship to God is possible because He is a real Person—who made us in His own image!

Questions to Ponder

1. What does it mean to be a person?
2. Why are animals not persons?
3. What marks of personality does God have that you would especially find helpful?
4. In what ways were (and are) the emotions of God encouraging to you?
5. What do you believe is possible for us if God is a real Person?

4

Is There More Than One God?

That question was asked of me in Tokyo, Japan, where I spoke on the existence of God to an audience composed primarily of Buddhists. The word *God* was not understood by them in the context in which I was using it. They were very confused over the Christian concept of the Trinity, which sounded to them like three gods. I used several illustrations and tried to answer their questions, but the confusion remained. Culturally, they were not raised in an atmosphere that exposed them to Christianity, and they found this concept most difficult to comprehend.

Perhaps you have also struggled with the Christian view of God—that He is three in one. Christians are often accused of believing in three gods. The word *Trinity* does not appear in the Bible, which nowhere teaches that there are three gods. There is only one God! But Christians do believe that God manifests Himself in three Persons. One God—three Persons—is that really possible?

We can illustrate this problem mathematically. By using the numeral "1" three times, we can come to two different conclusions: $1 + 1 + 1 = 3$ and $1 \times 1 \times 1 = 1$. The first formula results in a trinity; the second formula represents a tri-unity. The word *tri-unity* is a more proper term than *trinity* when explaining the nature of God. He is three in one—or one in three respects.

People have used various illustrations to reveal the essential nature of God. Some use the egg with its yolk, white, and shell.

But the yolk is neither the shell nor the white, and in that respect, the egg is an inadequate illustration. Some use water (H_2O) which can appear as a gas, liquid, or solid (ice). Others use a triangle with its three sides. Such illustrations may help us see the possibility of how one can be three or three be one, but they all fall short of giving us adequate information on the nature of God as described in the Bible.

Sometimes we must believe when we do not fully understand. Our minds are finite, and God is infinite. We can never fully comprehend His Person or greatness. There are many things we believe in yet do not understand or see with our eyes (electricity, wind, radio waves, and so on).

God Is One

Sometimes when stating an important truth, we ignore another equally important truth and become unbalanced in our understanding. Before we try to tackle the difficult problem of the tri-unity of God, let us start with the unity of God. The Bible does teach that God is one, and that He is the only God.

In Deuteronomy, we read that "the LORD Himself is God; there is none other besides Him. . . . The LORD Himself is God in heaven above and on the earth beneath; there is no other" (Deuteronomy 4:35, 39). If you are Jewish, you are very familiar with the words of Deuteronomy 6:4: "Hear, O Israel: The LORD our God, the LORD is one!" The word for "one" in Hebrew also occurs in Genesis 2:24, where man and woman are called "one flesh." Obviously, there is some sense in which two can be one, since man and woman are one flesh. Because God is one, it does not necessarily demand that He cannot also be two or three. He is one in some sense, but can be two or three in another sense or respect.

Isaiah 44:6 is an interesting verse. Two Persons are called "Jehovah" in that verse. The first Jehovah is called "the King of Israel." The second Jehovah (Lord of hosts) is called the "Redeemer." To be more specific, the Redeemer is called "*his* Redeemer," namely, the one who belongs to the King of Israel. The verse continues: "I am the First and I am the Last; Besides Me there is no God." Verse 8 asks, "Is there a God besides Me? Indeed there is no other Rock; I know not one." The King of Israel is called "the First and . . . the Last." It is most interesting to note that in Revelation 1:17, Jesus Christ refers to Himself as "the First and the Last."

Isaiah 45:5 adds: "I am the LORD, and there is no other; There is no God besides Me." Verse 6 says that "there is none besides Me. I am the LORD, and there is no other."

Jesus Himself agreed with the teaching that God is one. In Mark 12:29, He responded to a scribe's question about which commandment is the foremost of all by quoting Deuteronomy 6:4: "Hear, O Israel, the LORD our God, the LORD is one." In John 5:44, Jesus said, "How can you believe . . . and do not seek the honor that comes from the only God." And yet He also said: "I and My Father are one." The Jews, knowing that the Old Testament teaches the unity and uniqueness of God, picked up stones to stone Him to death for blasphemy. They understood His words to be making Himself equal with God.

The Apostle Paul taught the unity of God:

> Therefore concerning the eating of things offered to idols, we know that an idol is nothing in the world, and that *there is no other God but one*. For even if there are so-called gods, whether in heaven or on earth (as there are many gods and many lords), yet for us there is only one God, the Father, of whom are all things, and we for Him; and one Lord Jesus Christ, through whom are all things, and through whom we live.
>
> 1 Corinthians 8:4–6

James 2:19 adds, "You believe that there is one God. You do well. Even the demons believe—and tremble!" The demons of hell are smarter than many people! They do not doubt that God is one. They know He exists and that He is the only real God there is. They tremble before Him!

Because God is one, we are assured that He has one plan of salvation that includes all people:

> Or is He the God of the Jews only? Is He not also the God of the Gentiles? Yes, of the Gentiles also, since there is one God who will justify the circumcised by faith and the uncircumcised through faith.
>
> Romans 3:29–30

There is not a separate God for Gentiles, and another one for Jews. There is only one God. There cannot be any other claim upon the human heart. That is why the Bible follows the statement of God's unity with the exhortation to love God with all of our heart, soul, mind, and strength (Deuteronomy 6:4–5).

The one and only God is supposedly worshiped by all religious peoples of the world. However, when we observe such worship up close, we often discover that the beliefs about this one and only God are quite diverse. God is described and understood in ways that completely contradict the views of others. When pagan cultures decide that the one and only God they worship is one among many other gods that other cultures worship, they have just denied what they say they believe. Roman society was so confused about all the ideas and concepts of God that they allowed a polytheistic view (many gods) to be official policy.

The Bible teaches that God is one—and that there is no other god besides Him. That particular position becomes the basis for all future discussions about God. Is the Bible correct? Is its view and statements about God the only correct position on this matter? The Bible does not allow for alternate viewpoints. We either agree or we prove it to be wrong.

The Bible's Teaching About the Nature of God

Jewish people believe (as do Christians) that God is one and there is only one God. They often state that the idea of the tri-unity of God comes from pagan culture and Gentile influence, not from the Bible.

My wife and I lived for several years in an Orthodox Jewish neighborhood. Our next-door neighbors were so highly dedicated to all their Jewish traditions and beliefs that they seemed isolated most of the time and did not want their children to play with ours. One day, our youngest son came home and told us that his Jewish neighbor (his own age) told him he could not play with him because we were idolaters. He thought that we believed in three gods, and that would make us pagans in his eyes. He was not to associate with people who believed such things. We had some explaining to do that day with our son!

The Name of God Is a Plural Noun!

The Hebrew word for "God" is *elohim*. The words *el* and *elohe* can also mean "God," but are in the singular form rather than the plural. The plural form is used hundreds of times in the Bible. When referring to pagan "gods," the word is *elohim,* and the same word is used of the one and only God. While this does not prove much, it is very interesting in its implication about the nature of God Himself. It is possible to argue that God is more than one, even though He is one in some sense.

Plural Pronouns Are Used of God!

If the word *God* referred only to a single Person, then how do we explain the plural pronouns that are used in the following passages?

Genesis 1:26—"Then God said, 'Let *Us* make man in *Our* image. . . .'"

Genesis 3:22—"Then the LORD God said, 'Behold, the man has become like one of *Us*. . . .'"

Genesis 11:6–7—"And the LORD said. . . . 'Come, let *Us* go down. . . .'"

Isaiah 6:8—"Also I heard the voice of the Lord, saying:

'Whom shall I send, And who will go for *Us*?' "

To whom is God talking when He says, "Let *Us* make man in *Our* image"?

One religious group teaches that God was discussing this with the angels, and that man is therefore made in the image of God *and* the angels. But if that is the meaning of these passages, why is the phrase "to the angels" not in the text? And how do we explain Isaiah 6:8, where the Lord says, "Whom shall *I* send, And who will go for *Us*?" He certainly was not speaking about the angels when He said "I."

Previous to the creation of man, God was able to talk with Himself. God was referring to Himself as "Us." If God is more than one, the use of plural pronouns is understandable.

God's Name Is Applied to More Than One Person in the Same Text!

> Your throne, O God, is forever and ever; A scepter of righteousness is the scepter of Your kingdom. You love righteousness and hate wickedness; Therefore God, Your God, has anointed You With the oil of gladness more than Your companions.
>
> Psalm 45:6–7

The first "God" has a *scepter* and a *kingdom*. This "God" also has a "God" who has anointed Him above all others.

In Isaiah 48:12–16, we have a fascinating passage dealing with the tri-unity of God and the fact that His name is applied to more than one Person in the same text or passage. In verse 12, the One who is speaking says, "I am He, I am the First, I am also the Last." That phrase is used of the Lord Himself (Isaiah 41:4; 44:6). Yet, in Isaiah 48:16, this Lord says, "And now the LORD GOD and His Spirit Have sent Me." We have two Jehovahs (the word *Lord*) in the same passage, completely distinct from each other.

In Psalm 110:1, it says, "The LORD said to my Lord." In

Matthew 22:41–46, Jesus refers to this passage and presents the difficulty of the "son of David" being called David's "Lord."

The Bible presents information on the tri-unity of God, if we are willing to examine the evidence without bias and prejudice. There are ways to get around each of these "problem texts" if one is so inclined, but it never seems to answer the questions. It only ignores the obvious facts and seeks to interpret loosely rather than literally. The truth is, the Bible proves rather conclusively that God is more than One!

Three Persons Are Each Recognized as "God"!

Contrary to what many people think, the New Testament is rather silent about the heavenly Father being called "God." It is often assumed that the reader understands that fact. There is one passage, however, that is quite clear. In John 6:27, Jesus says, "Do not labor for the food which perishes, but for the food which endures to everlasting life, which the Son of Man will give you, because God the Father has set His seal on Him." Obviously, the Father is called "God" in that verse.

The "Son" of the "Father" is called "God" in Hebrews 1:8 (which is a quotation from Psalm 45:6–7): "But to the Son He says: 'Your throne, O God, is forever and ever.'" The Father calls the Son "O God." One translation of that verse by a religious group that denies the deity of Jesus Christ reads: "God is My throne." However, the manuscript evidence is against such a rendering. In John 1:1 we read: ". . . and the Word was God." Verse 14 of that same chapter says: "And the Word became flesh and dwelt among us." Jesus is *the Word,* and He is called "God." In Romans 9:5, the Messiah is called "the eternally blessed God." In Acts 20:28, Paul instructs the elders of the church at Ephesus "to shepherd the church of God which He purchased with His own blood." Notice carefully that *God* is described as the One who "purchased with His own blood." Of course, it was Jesus who shed His blood on the cross. This verse teaches that Jesus is God, and Jesus Christ is called "the true God and eternal life" (1 John 5:20).

The Holy Spirit is also called "God" in the New Testament. Peter asked Ananias, "Why has Satan filled your heart to lie to the Holy Spirit?. . . . You have not lied to men but to God" (Acts 5:3, 4). Obviously, the Holy Spirit is referred to as "God" in that text.

I came home from the office one day to have lunch with my wife, only to discover that we had company. Two men in white shirts, dark pants, and long ties, were talking to my wife about God. They had lots of books on the table, and their bicycles were parked out front. My wife offered them some of her best cookies and something to drink. When I walked into the living room, they both seemed excited that I had come home and were anxious to share their beliefs with me.

I listened as they tried to explain that Jesus Christ is not called "God" in the Bible. It seems my wife had already told them that she believed that Jesus Christ was and is God in human flesh. I shared some of the verses with them that are listed above, and one of the gentlemen (obviously the trainee) asked his partner: "Why didn't you tell me about these verses?" He quickly said, "We'll talk about it later." As I continued to press the point about the trinity of God, the trainer said to his trainee, "It's time to go!" I invited them to come back, but they never returned!

Each of the three Persons is clearly distinguished from the other two. The name *God* is applied to the Father, Son, and the Holy Spirit, but that does not make them one and the same. They are separated from each other, even though they are all called "God." In John 14:16, we read: "And I [Jesus] will pray the Father, and He will give you another Helper [Holy Spirit], that He may abide with you forever." The Father, in giving the Holy Spirit to us, is thus separated from the Holy Spirit. Jesus is also separated from the Father in that He asks the Father to give the Holy Spirit. Jesus and the Father are not one and the same (as some religious groups teach). They communicate with each other. The same idea is found in John 14:26: "But the Helper, the Holy Spirit, whom the Father will send in My name, He will teach you all things, and bring to your remembrance all things that I said to you.'' Jesus also said, ''But when the Helper comes, whom I shall send to you from the Father, the Spirit of truth who proceeds from the Father, He will testify of Me'' (John 15:26).

In Matthew 3:16–17, all three Persons are mentioned, yet are quite distinct from each other. *Jesus* is being baptized in water by John the Baptist. The *Father* is in the heavens, saying, ''This is My beloved Son.'' And the *Holy Spirit* descends as a dove to land upon Jesus.

Three Persons are set forth as one God, not three Gods. In John 10:30, Jesus said, ''I and My Father are one.'' Some religious groups teach that this merely means ''one in purpose.'' However, the Jews who heard that statement thought otherwise: ''The Jews took up stones again to stone Him'' (verse 31). When Jesus questioned their action, they said that they were stoning Him ''for blasphemy, and because You, being a Man, make Yourself God'' (verse 33). They understood His remark as meaning that He and the Father were one in the sense that they were both God.

The Father and the Spirit are seen as one in 1 Corinthians 2:11, in that they know each other's thoughts: ''Even so no one knows the things of God except the Spirit of God.'' The Son and the Spirit appear as one in Romans 8:9: ''But you are not in the flesh but in the Spirit, if indeed the Spirit of God dwells in you. Now if anyone does not have the Spirit of Christ, he is not His.'' The Spirit of God in the believer is called the ''Spirit of Christ.''

A very interesting passage in this regard is found in John 14. In verse 16, Jesus promises to ask the Father and He will give the Spirit to be in the believers forever. In verse 18, Jesus says, ''I will not leave you orphans; I will come to you.'' In verse 16, it is the Holy Spirit who comes, but in verse 18, it is Jesus who comes. Then, in verse 23, Jesus says, ''If anyone loves Me, he will keep My word; and My Father will love him, and We will come to him, and make Our home with him.'' In verse 16, the Spirit comes; in verse 18, Jesus comes; and in verse 23, the Father comes along with Jesus, and they make their abode in the believer. What a fantastic truth!

Illustrations are inadequate in describing the nature of God, but the Bible is clear on one thing: God is not one and three in the same sense. God is one in terms of essence, substance, or being. God is three in terms of personality and function.

But How Can . . . ?

While sitting on the grass in a park, I started thinking about the tri-unity of God. I picked a three-leaf clover and started to analyze the problem. Here was one stem and three leaves. But the stem was not the same as the leaf! Could I honestly say that all three leaves had one stem? Yes. There was something about that three-leaf clover that reminded me of the nature of God.

Water (H_2O) is also a reminder to me of the possibility of the tri-unity of God. First I boiled some water on the stove and watched the steam rise. Then I took an ice cube out of the refrigerator and laid it on the stove beside the boiling water. Here were steam, liquid water, and ice—but all three were composed of exactly the same elements. They were just appearing in different forms.

When I came to God, there were some questions. God is one, and yet three Persons are called "God." Not easy to understand! My greatest difficulties came in dealing with three important questions, all related to the argument about Jesus being called God.

1. *How can Jesus be the Son of God and also be called "God" at the same time?* I was troubled by the word *Son*. It suggests that He was born and had a beginning. Since God is eternal and does not have a beginning or end, how could Jesus be God?

My sons are certainly a part of me. Genetically, they are related to me. They have certain of my physical features and (hopefully!) some from my wife. My sons are not me, but we are one in the sense that we are all human and they are the result of the sexual union of my wife and me.

Most of my conflict over this problem can be related to my understanding (or misunderstanding) of the word *Son*. To me this implies a child born of His parents. He would have had a point in time where He began to exist. But God has always existed—

therefore, how could Jesus be God? The answer is found in the original language of the New Testament—Greek.

The word *Son,* as used of Jesus Christ, is a special word that does not refer to birth or origin. The Greek word (*huios*) refers to an heir, one who will receive the inheritance of the Father. It does not imply birth. As a matter of fact, the word for a child born to his parents (*teknos*) is never used of Jesus Christ. A "son" (heir) could be an adopted son; even a servant in the household whom the father would desire to honor could be a "son."

When Jesus was born of the virgin Mary, He had no human father. His conception was caused by the miraculous power of God the Holy Spirit, according to Luke 1:34–35. John 1:2 says of Jesus: "He was in the beginning with God." When speaking of His birth into the human family, the Bible uses distinct and concise terms to indicate His preexistence. In John 1:14, it says that He "became flesh." The Greek word implies a change of condition, not a new beginning.

2. How can Jesus be called the "only begotten Son" of God if He is really God? The phrase *only begotten* is used by the Apostle John in his writings on five occasions to refer to Jesus Christ. In John 1:18, we read: "No one has seen God at any time. The only begotten Son, who is in the bosom of the Father, He has declared Him." The phrase *only begotten* does make you think! How can God, who never had a beginning or end, be called "only begotten"? John 3:16 says that God gave His "only begotten Son." John 1:14 refers to Jesus as the "only begotten of the Father." John 3:18 says He is the "only begotten son of God," and 1 John 4:9 also refers to Him as the "only begotten Son."

The answer to this problem lies in the use of the phrase *only begotten* in Hebrews 11:17. Isaac is referred to as Abraham's "only begotten son." Abraham had other children than Isaac (Genesis 16:15; 25:1–2). In what sense was Isaac the "only begotten"? Hebrews 11:18 gives the answer: It was through Isaac that the Messiah would come, and God would fulfill His promise to Abraham. In that sense, Isaac is the *unique* son of Abraham, not the only child ever born of Abraham. Jesus is the *unique* Son of God. There is no one like Him or equal to Him.

3. *If Jesus is God, why did He submit to the will of His Father?* There are many statements of Christ that indicate His complete submission to the will of His Father, His subordination to the Father's authority. Jesus willingly accepted certain limitations to His nature and Person when He became man. He laid aside His divine rights and privileges in order to redeem us. The work of incarnation (becoming flesh) and redemption necessitated His submission and subordination to the Father. Philippians 2:5–8 brings this out in some detail. It is clear that Jesus existed in the very form (Greek: *morphe*) of God. That is, He had God's essential nature. But Philippians 2:7 says He "made Himself of no reputation." He did this by humbling Himself and becoming obedient even to the point of His death on the cross. But He did all of this voluntarily. Jesus said:

> "Therefore My Father loves Me, because I lay down My life that I may take it again. No one takes it from Me, but I lay it down of Myself. I have power to lay it down, and I have power to take it again. This command I have received from My Father."
>
> John 10:17–18

Jesus was in complete control of the situation surrounding His death and resurrection. He was not a helpless victim. During the days of His flesh, He willingly accepted His role of complete submission to the will of the Father. Therefore, He could (and did) say that the Father "is greater than all" (John 10:29).

Why Is It Necessary to Believe in the Tri-Unity of God?

I was teaching a class on the nature and existence of God and drew a triangle on the chalkboard. Inside the triangle (which I labeled "God"), I drew three circles for Father, Son, and Holy Spirit. The three circles did not intersect each other. I then drew a box around the circle with the name "Son" in it, and I proceeded to explain to the class that the triangle represented the one and only

God with all of His attributes and characteristics. I also shared that the circles represented personality, and that there were three distinct and separate Persons, each bearing all the attributes of God. Finally, I explained that the box represented a physical body, and that Jesus, the Son, was the only Person of the Godhead to become flesh.

As soon as I finished, a student raised his hand and asked, "What difference does it really make to believe that God is three and one at the same time?" A good question! I gave him three answers—I'm sure there are more.

1. *Without the tri-unity of God, it is difficult to see how we could have a God of eternal love.* Love demands an object to be loved. God is eternal. Before man was created, whom did God love? How can the eternal nature of love operate if there was no object to be loved? Some answer, "God loved Himself." Others say, "God loved others in His mind before they were created." That is possible, but in terms of the object's experiencing that love, it is impossible. If God's love demands that someone other than Himself be loved, then—prior to creation—His love is not functioning as it should. Naturally, we have entered a realm of thinking that puts a strain upon the finite mind, since it is difficult to comprehend how God's love functions now, let alone before creation!

If you believe in the tri-unity of God, you have no problem on this point. The Father loved the Son, and the Son loved the Father and the Spirit, and the Spirit loved the Father and the Son.

2. *Without the tri-unity of God, we have no complete revelation of God.* Only God can reveal God completely. If Jesus is God, then it is quite understandable to read John 1:18: "No one has seen God at any time. The only begotten Son, who is in the bosom of the Father, He has declared Him." Jesus has put Him on display! In John 14:8, Philip says, "Lord, show us the Father, and it is sufficient for us." Jesus replies, "Have I been with you so long, and yet you have not known Me, Philip? He who has seen Me has seen the Father; so how can you say, 'Show us the Father'?" (verse 9). When you see Jesus, you see the Father. God reveals God, and Jesus is the final revelation of God:

God, who at various times and in different ways spoke in time past to the fathers by the prophets, has in these last days spoken to us by His Son, whom He has appointed heir of all things, through whom also He made the worlds; who being the brightness of His glory and the express image of His person, and upholding all things by the word of His power, when He had by Himself purged our sins, sat down at the right hand of the Majesty on high.

Hebrews 1:1–3

3. *Without the tri-unity of God, there can be no salvation from sin.* In Mark 2:1–12, Jesus heals a paralytic man. In the process of healing him, Jesus says, "Son, your sins are forgiven you." The scribes who were there said that Jesus was blaspheming. Their argument was centered in their question, "Who can forgive sins but God alone?" They were correct: Only God can forgive sin. If Jesus is God, then He can forgive us. If He is not God, then we have no salvation from sin through Him. But 2 Corinthians 5:19 says that "God was in Christ reconciling the world to Himself."

How important is it to believe in the tri-unity of God? "Every spirit that confesses that Jesus Christ has come in the flesh is of God, and every spirit that does not confess that Jesus Christ has come in the flesh is not of God. . . ." (1 John 4:2–3). "For many deceivers have gone out into the world who do not confess Jesus Christ as coming in the flesh. This is a deceiver and an antichrist" (2 John 7). Verse 9 adds, "Whoever transgresses and does not abide in the doctrine of Christ does not have God. He who abides in the doctrine of Christ has both the Father and the Son."

To be a Christian, you must believe that Jesus Christ is God who has come in the flesh. If Jesus is not God, then He cannot save you from your sin. If He is merely man, then He is a sinner, and needs a Saviour Himself. If He was a perfect man, but only a man, He could substitute His life for only one other person. Only God could substitute His infinite life for the sum total of all who believe in Him. The only way we can be true Christians is by believing that Jesus Christ is God in human flesh—the God-Man, our only Saviour from sin.

Questions to Ponder

1. What illustrations would you use to explain the tri-unity of God?

2. Why is it important to believe that God is one and the only God?

3. What evidences from the Bible do we have that would indicate God as more than one Person?

4. How can Jesus be God and the Son of God at the same time?

5. What does "only begotten" mean?

6. Why is it important to believe in the tri-unity of God?

5

When Was God Born?

Our visit to London was thoroughly enjoyable, but our conversations with people on the streets were most perplexing. This proud British nation, once the center of the missionary movement that spread the gospel of Jesus Christ around the world, now seemed quite unaware of its roots. One dignified gentleman who enjoyed a bit of conversation with a religious fanatic from America (me) was quite interested in my viewpoints about God. He reasoned, "Everything has a beginning and an end; so, when did your God begin?"

I have thought about that question a great deal since. It must seem strange to nonreligious people to believe that someone who created the heavens and the earth never had a point in time in which He Himself began to exist. Christians, Jews, and many other religious people believe that God is eternal. He never had a beginning and He will never have an end. Is that possible? Is that consistent with the facts as we know them?

Does not everything have a beginning? I do my thinking from start to finish, from beginning to end. It is hard for me to conceive of something or someone who has always been there and never had a point of beginning. But that is exactly what the Bible teaches about God! He is eternal—no beginning or end. I know the date of my birth, even though I did not have that understanding at the moment it happened. There was a time when I was not around, and my mother remembers that fact—I don't! God has always been there.

When we talk of eternity, we usually think of it in terms of time. According to the Bible, God made time. He is above it and controlling it. One day He will get rid of time—no more watches and clocks! When I think about things, I see them in perspective to time, the sequence of events, from start to finish. I have trouble thinking about eternity and don't really understand it. I doubt if it is possible for me to comprehend it in my present frame of mind.

Several years ago, my youngest child came up to me and asked, "Dad, were you ever a baby?" Though amused at his question, I realized his problem. He had never known me as a baby and had questions about whether I was ever as small as he was. Sometimes I feel that way in relation to God. The Bible says, however, that He was never born. He has always existed. I find security in that truth, even though I don't fully understand it.

What Do We Mean By "Eternal"?

When we speak of the "eternal" God, what do we mean? Someone who has lasted a long time? Yes, but much more than that. Our family was waiting to be seated at a local restaurant. It was crowded, and we had already waited about forty minutes. My youngest son said, "Dad, they're taking forever to seat us!" In his eyes, eternity is at least forty minutes long!

"Eternal" means at least two things in reference to God:

• God has no beginning or end.
• God cannot be measured or controlled by time.

He created time itself and sees before and beyond its parameters. God is not controlled by the sequence of events—He doesn't need a watch or a calendar.

Biblical Words That Mean "Eternal" . . .

Seven Hebrew words are translated "eternal" or "forever" in the Old Testament, and three Greek words are used in the New

Testament. Each of these words contributes to our understanding of the eternal nature of God. The following chart might help you in any further study of the subject:

Old Testament Words	Usage (No. of times)	Meaning	Examples
NETSACH	34	Completeness	God's anger Psalm 103:9 God's presence Psalm 16:11
AD	48	Longlasting	God's guidance Psalm 48:14 God's throne Psalm 45:6
QEDEM	60	Ancient; Old	Eternal God Deuteronomy 33:27 Habakkuk 1:12
OREC	93	Length (no limits)	Believer in God's house Psalm 23:6 God's holiness Psalm 93:5
TAMID	103	Continuity or Perpetuity	God's eyes on Israel's land Deuteronomy 11:12 David's sin Psalm 51:3
DOR	129	Dependability	God's covenant Genesis 9:12 God's counsel Psalm 33:11
OLAM	400	Everlasting; Unending	God's protection Deuteronomy 33:27 God's lovingkindness Psalm 100:5 God Himself Genesis 21:33 Psalm 90:2

New Testament Words	Usage (No. of times)	Meaning	Examples
AIDIOS	2	Continuous	God's power Romans 1:20 Chains of darkness Jude 6
AIONIOS	6	Unending	Eternal life John 3:16 God's covenant Hebrews 13:20 God Himself Romans 16:26
AION	100	Endless period of time	God's Word 1 Peter 1:23, 25 God's throne Hebrews 1:8 God's life Revelation 4:10 Jesus Christ Hebrews 13:8

The grand total of these seven Hebrew words and three Greek words in terms of usage in the Bible amounts to over 1,000 times. Obviously, the word *eternal* is a very important word. To say that God is eternal is to affect a multitude of issues, doctrines, and facts about which the Bible speaks. It affects our own understanding of the origin of all things and the control of events, and gives a unique view of history that removes doubt and uncertainty. God's eternal nature brings stability and meaning to your life and provides wonderful security.

When our children were quite young, we were trying to teach them about God. It was not easy, as many of you parents already know. My little girl wanted Daddy to explain what "forever" means. I looked at my wife and she said, "She's *your* daughter!" Here's what I tried to tell my family that day—maybe it will help you.

1. Before time began, God existed! Genesis 1:1 says, "In the beginning [a word of time] God created the heavens and the earth.'' When things began, God was there already—He caused them to happen.

To say that God is eternal involves some important teaching about God's relationship to time. We are creatures of time, controlled by it. We cannot live yesterday nor tomorrow. Today is all we have. The moment in which I just wrote that last sentence is now gone. Time implies a beginning and an end. Time is divided by God into various units of measurement, such as years, months, days, hours, minutes, seconds, and so on. Why are there 24 hours in a day and not 30? Why not 1,000 days in a year, instead of the usual 365 (with a break every four years!)? Calendars have not always been the same, although they were originally determined by the moon. But even then there was a fixed order, a finished design. Time was established, and it moves on, and man cannot do anything about it! Genesis 1:14 says, ''Then God said, 'Let there be lights in the firmament of the heavens to divide the day from the night; and let them be for signs and seasons, and for days and years.''' There you have it—time!

To say that God is eternal means that He was there before time. In Volume 1 of the commentary *Bereishis* (Genesis), published by Mesorah Publications of New York, we have this interesting statement on page 2 of the section entitled, ''An Overview—Creation'':

> Prior to creation there was nothing save the glory of God. Nothing—it is a concept that we, creatures in a physical world, cannot even begin to comprehend, just as the blind cannot comprehend the sunset and the deaf a symphony. Can we conceive of a world without time or space? We can speak of it, think of it, but the truth is that we cannot really imagine phenomena so foreign to our experience.*

Many people will not believe this fact of the Bible. They cannot

---

Bereishis (Genesis), Vol. 1, p. 2 (New York: Mesorah Publications, Ltd., 1977). Translation and commentary by Rabbi Meir Zlotowitz.

accept the sublime simplicity of the opening phrase of the Bible: "In the beginning God. . . ." The Bible says that it is a matter of faith:

> By faith we understand that the worlds were prepared by the word of God, so that the things which are seen were not made of things which are visible.
>
> Hebrews 11:3

Let's face it—you cannot prove whether this is true or false by any known scientific method. Did everything "just happen" (including time)? When you start to think seriously about this universe, you inevitably come up against the problem of origin. How did it all begin? The Bible makes it simple for you: It starts with God, who had no beginning or end. He is the foundation upon which everything and everyone is built. God is eternal, and that means He was there before time began.

2. God exists in the past, present, and future at the same moment of time! This point is not simply that God continues as long as time does. It is saying that the presence and existence of God encompass all that time represents in the past, present, and future. God is not limited or controlled by it. He exists (presently) in all of it (past, present, and future). Jesus referred to this attribute of God when He said: "Before Abraham was [came into being], I AM" (John 8:58). It takes a little time to comprehend that statement! Jesus did *not* say, "Before Abraham was, I was." That would be true, but it would not contain all of the truth. "I AM" is far different from "I was."

My understanding of this doctrine (very limited—of course) is that presently, at this very moment, God exists, and at the same time He exists at the time of Abraham and at the time of His future kingdom on earth. His presence fills it all, and His nature transcends its dimensions. I do not understand how that is possible, but I believe that is what the Bible teaches.

Revelation 4:8 proclaims: "Holy, holy, holy, Lord God Almighty, Who was and is and is to come!" God has always existed and always will, and His perspective of things is not controlled by the past or the future. He sees it all in any one moment of time. That is how God was able to show the future to the Apostle John in A.D. 90 on the isle of Patmos in the Mediterranean Sea. These events that are now recorded in the Book of Revelation still lie in the future. They have not yet happened, but in God's mind and plan, they already have. John recorded the words of Jesus Christ in Revelation 22 (the last chapter of the Bible) as: "I am the Alpha and the Omega [first and last letters of the Greek alphabet], the Beginning and the End, the First and the Last" (verse 13).

One afternoon, while I was enjoying a pro football game on television, one of my children became fascinated with instant replays. After a play had been completed, the television cameras would take us back in time and let us watch it over again (tough on the referees!). My son asked, "Is that what God can do, Dad?" I asked, "Do what, son?" He explained, "See the past when you're still in the present." As I heard him say that, I thought about the eternal nature of God. God's mind is an instant-replay machine for any past or future event.

3. God dwells outside of time and is not limited by it!

> For thus says the high and exalted One who lives forever, whose name is Holy: "I dwell on a high and holy place, and also With the contrite and lowly in spirit, in order to revive the spirit of the lowly, And to revive the heart of the contrite."
>
> Isaiah 57:15, NASB

He is the *high and exalted One*. Psalm 90:4 also suggests this truth: "For a thousand years in Your sight Are like yesterday when it is past, And like a watch in the night." And 2 Peter 3:8 adds that "with the Lord one day is as a thousand years, and a thousand years as one day." God is not a victim of the clock. Time is something He invented and He controls. The psalmist pictured the eternal God as being outside of time when he wrote: "Your eyes saw my substance, being yet unformed, And in Your book they all were written, The days fashioned for me, When as yet there were none of them'' (Psalm 139:16). God is on the outside, fully knowledgeable of everything time will bring. All of our days are known to Him before we experience them.

There is great freedom when you are not controlled by time or limited by it. When people say, "Take your time," it may or may not mean exactly what they said. There have been occasions when I was not aware of time. I was working on a project one day and completely forgot about what time it was or what time I had used in accomplishing the task. I was just enjoying myself. However, when it became dark outside, I finally became aware of time.

God is not limited by time—He has no deadlines to meet other than what He Himself has established for us and which He Himself controls. Because He dwells outside of our time frame, He can see clearly what our tomorrows are like and what our yesterdays have been. What marvelous perspective that gives Him!

4. God is the Author of time!

> [God] has in these last days spoken to us by His Son, whom He has appointed heir of all things, through whom also He made the worlds.
>
> Hebrews 1:2

Who made time? God did. He made the ages of time. He established them. Isaiah 9:6 calls the Messiah the "Everlasting Father." Time was begun, designed, and controlled by God Almighty. That, of course, has serious implications in our lives. What happens today is not by accident or coincidence, for there is a plan that has been established by God.

Acts 17:26 is one fascinating verse which refers to God as the Author of time. Paul is preaching at Athens and speaks of the sovereignty and control of God over the affairs of men: "And He has made from one blood every nation of men to dwell on all the face of the earth, and has *determined their preappointed times* and the boundaries of their habitation." This means that the nations of the world are controlled by God. He predetermined how long they would be in power. Their times are in God's hands! That is very comforting when you take a good long look at human history, especially the history of nations and empires.

5. God is controlling time! Thomas Jefferson, who had such an important role in the development of American life and beliefs in terms of government and politics, was a committed deist. Yet, in his view of God, events and circumstances are not controlled by God. He believed that God's relationship to all things was something like winding a clock and letting it run down. God was helpless to change things and not personally involved.

The Bible, however, teaches just the opposite. God is controlling time itself and the sequence of events, which includes all the days of man's life. Psalm 139:16 says that God's eyes see a man's "unformed substance" and that the days of his life are all written in God's book before any of them come to pass.

According to Hebrews 9:27, the day of our death is a divine appointment. In this sense, everyone dies on time, since the day when each of us will die is determined by God. The so-called accidental death is not really an accident at all. The means of death will vary, but when it is time, nothing will change it. The important thing is to be ready!

A little boy was sitting in front of a huge grandfather's clock waiting for it to strike twelve. He loved to hear the chimes of this clock ring its twelve times, one for each hour completed. As he listened—"one, two, three, four . . . eleven, twelve"—all of a sudden something broke in the mechanism of that clock and the chimes continued—"thirteen, fourteen"—and so on. The boy became frightened and ran to his mother in the kitchen, shouting, "Mother, Mother, it's later than it's ever been before!" With each passing day, we are one day closer to our death. Are you ready?

The Bible also teaches that the day and hour of the second coming of Christ has already been set by God. Jesus says: "But of that day and hour no one knows, no, not even the angels of heaven, but My Father only" (Matthew 24:36). Acts 1:7 says that the "times" and "seasons" are in the Father's control.

One of the amazing statements concerning how God is controlling events is found in Daniel 2:21: "And He changes the times and the seasons; He removes kings and raises up kings." Political changes are in the hands of God, whether by popular election, military coup, or royal descent. The means used is unimportant, since God is in control. All of the events of history are being operated by God Himself, who is bringing them all to a grand conclusion which He alone has designed!

Five biblical concepts formulate what we believe about God when we say He is eternal.

1. Before time began, God existed.
2. God exists in the past, present, and future at the same moment of time.
3. God dwells outside of time and is not limited by it.
4. God is the Author of time.
5. God is controlling time.

That which is eternal is so because God is eternal. His name is eternal because He is eternal. The Psalmist says, "Your name, O Lord, endures forever" (Psalm 135:13). His Word is eternal, according to Psalm 119:89, 152, 160. Isaiah 40:8 states that "the grass withers, the flower fades, but the word of our God stands forever." Many things such as His covenant, throne, kingdom, and purpose will endure forever because God Himself is eternal.

The everlasting God manifests many attributes and characteristics which are said to be eternal. His righteousness, power, ways, love, and salvation are all eternal, according to the Bible. Psalm 103:17 says, "But the mercy of the LORD is from everlasting to everlasting." God's response to us is not given out of limited resources. He is eternal. Most things in our lives are so temporary and transitory. God is not, and that makes a world of difference in terms of my response to Him.

What Difference Does It Make?

Is it important to believe that God had no beginning or end? Does His eternal nature affect us in any way? If you don't believe in God, what possible difference would it make?

To Non-Believers with Love . . .

If you are not a believer in Jesus Christ, the logical conclusions of the eternal nature and character of God are indeed frightening. The Bible teaches that you have no excuse before God if you ignore the truth of His eternal power in the material universe which He has created (Romans 1:20). Creation does not reveal everything about God, but one thing should be obvious: Whoever made it had to exist before it was made and, therefore, is eternal.

The most serious fact facing the unbeliever in knowing that God is eternal is that the consequences of not believing in Jesus Christ are eternal, not temporary. Matthew 25:46 speaks of "everlasting punishment" as well as "eternal life." In this verse, the same adjective (*aionion*) modifies both "punishment" and "life." Many people like to believe that the only punishment they will experience is the trouble of this life, but the Bible teaches otherwise. Punishment will last forever!

In 2 Thessalonians 1:7–9, we are told that when Jesus Christ returns to this earth, He will judge "those who do not obey the gospel of our Lord Jesus Christ," and they will "be punished with everlasting [*aionion*] destruction from the presence of the Lord and from the glory of His power." Revelation 20:10 states that the devil, the beast (coming world ruler), and the false prophet (world religious leader) will be cast into the lake of fire. That torment in the lake of fire is described as being "day and night forever and ever." Verse 15 of that same chapter adds, "And anyone not found written in the Book of Life was cast into the lake of fire." Yes, the consequences of rejecting Jesus Christ as your Lord and Savior are everlasting! Because God is eternal and His plan is eternal, so are the consequences upon non-believers eternal.

To the Believer with Love . . .

Because God is eternal, we who believe in His Son, Jesus Christ, as our only Savior from sin will live forever. Jesus says, "Most assuredly, I say to you, he who hears My word and believes in Him who sent Me has *everlasting life,* and shall not come into judgment, but has passed from death into life'' (John 5:24). Eternal life is the present possession of every believer in Jesus Christ. It is not simply something you are going to receive in the future. You have it right now if you have Jesus! Daniel 12:2 states, ''And many of those who sleep in the dust of the earth shall awake, Some to *everlasting life,* Some to shame and everlasting contempt.''

One of the most wonderful promises in this regard is:

> And this is the testimony: that God has given us *eternal life,* and this life is in His Son. He who has the Son has life; he who does not have the Son of God does not have life. These things I have written to you who believe in the name of the Son of God, that you may know that you have *eternal life. . . .*
>
> 1 John 5:11–13

Because He is eternal, we can count on Him to do what He has said. Psalm 105:8 says, ''He has remembered His covenant *forever,* the word which He commanded, for a thousand generations.'' The Psalmist adds: ''He has given food to those who fear Him; He will ever be mindful of His covenant'' (Psalm 111:5), and ''Your faithfulness endures to all generations; You established the earth, and it abides'' (Psalm 119:90).

The eternal nature of God makes His counsel completely trustworthy and far superior to any reasonings of men: ''The counsel of the LORD stands *forever,* The plans of His heart to all generations'' (Psalm 33:11). This counsel will guide believers through all the difficult experiences of their lives. Psalm 48:14 tells us: ''For this is God, Our God forever and ever; He will be our guide Even to death.'' It is the eternal God who brings such assurance. He will guide us through all our days. We can trust Him: ''The eternal God is your refuge, And underneath are the everlasting arms. . . .'' (Deuteronomy 33:27). Jesus said in Matthew 28:20: ''Lo, I am with you always, even to the end of the age.'' Hebrews 13:5 adds, ''I will never leave you nor forsake you.''

In speaking of God's keeping power over His people Israel, we read in Psalm 89:36–37: "His seed shall endure forever, And His throne as the sun before Me. It shall be established forever like the moon, Even like the faithful witness in the sky." Psalm 90:1 assures us: "LORD, You have been our dwelling place in all generations." What wonderful security! Psalm 91:9–10 adds: "Because you have made the LORD, who is my refuge, Even the Most High, your habitation, No evil shall befall you, Nor shall any plague come near your dwelling." God's protection and security are mentioned many times in the Scriptures. He will take care of us. We have no need to be afraid, for He is the eternal God!

> Have you not known? Have you not heard? The Everlasting God, the LORD, The Creator of the ends of the earth, Neither faints nor is weary. There is no searching of His understanding. He gives power to the weak, And to those who have no might He increases strength. Even the youths shall faint and be weary, And the young men shall utterly fall, But those who wait on the LORD Shall renew their strength; They shall mount up with wings like eagles, They shall run and not be weary, They shall walk and not faint.
>
> Isaiah 40:28–30

How we need that kind of strength! Though we get tired and weary, the *Everlasting God* never does!

Our security is found in complete trust and dependency upon the eternal God, our Rock. Because He is eternal, He is reliable and trustworthy, and you can always depend upon Him. He will never let you down. Peace is found in trusting Him, not yourself.

God is controlling time and is above time. He was there before the earth was formed. As He had no beginning, so He will have no end. No start or finish, no beginning or end—simply the God who is always there!

Questions to Ponder

1. What do we mean when we say that God is eternal?
2. What is God's relationship to time?

3. What evidence do we have that God is controlling time?

4. What effect does the eternal nature of God have upon the non-believer?

5. Why is the eternal nature of God a blessing to the believer?

6

Where Is God?

Imagine for a moment that the first forty years of your life included the best education money could buy, access to all the wealth you could ever want, and the potentiality of being the most powerful person on earth, ruling the greatest nation. Sound good? Next imagine that through one act of violence, you were forced to leave all of those advantages and spend the next forty years of your life taking care of sheep in the desert.

Now suppose that while you were out taking care of the sheep one day, you saw a desert bush on fire, although the bush did not seem to burn. Then imagine hearing a majestic voice, speaking from the burning bush and asking you to go back to the place where you grew up—the most powerful nation on earth—and demand that some three million people working as slaves for that nation should be released. You would probably begin doing exactly what Moses did over 3,000 years ago—start making excuses for why you cannot do that!

In that amazing moment of history, when Moses needed some reassurance of how he could possibly do what was being asked of him, he heard these words: "I will certainly be with you" (Exodus 3:2). God's presence was promised.

There are times in all of our lives when the only thing that brings us comfort is the fact that God is there. To know that He really exists, and that He is present with you, will take you through some tough times and difficult trials.

In the summer of 1964, I was scuba diving in beautiful Schroon Lake, New York. The tank of air on my back had no gauge, but I was assured that it was full of air. Unfortunately, it was not! About twenty feet below the surface of the water and a hundred yards from the shoreline, my air supply ran out—a case of instant panic! To this day, I am not sure how I was rescued, but I woke up on the shore with a crowd of people around me. What I do remember was my response to God when I became aware of the fact that my air supply was gone. I said, "God, if You are there, I could sure use Your help right now." Several verses ran quickly through my mind, such as "I will never leave you nor forsake you" (Hebrews 13:5), and "Lo, I am with you always, even to the end of the age" (Matthew 28:20). I was hoping that last verse did not mean the end of my earthly existence!

What amazed me was the peace and comfort that came over me in that situation. I knew that God was there, taking care of me. There was nothing to worry about, since I had made my peace with God many years before that event. I was ready to die and be in heaven with my Lord. As it turned out, I am still around. God's presence not only comforted me in a difficult situation, but it gave me a confidence that everything would be all right.

It is difficult to answer the question "Where is God?", when you cannot see God with your physical eyesight: "Now to the King eternal, immortal, *invisible,* to God who alone is wise, be honor and glory forever and ever. Amen" (1 Timothy 1:17). To ask "Where is God?" is similar to asking "Where is the universe?"

We have learned so far that God is a real Person who exists through all eternity. He has never had a beginning nor will He have an end. But where is He? Can we locate Him? Is there a place where He can be found? The Bible admonishes us quite frequently to seek for Him, but where do we start looking?

In theological terms, we are talking about the omnipresence of God, the fact that He is everywhere. You cannot run away from Him, nor hide from His presence. As Dr. Francis Schaeffer has put it, He is the "God who is there." Perhaps the finest statement in the Bible on God's omnipresence is found in the Book of Psalms:

> Where can I go from Your Spirit? Or where can I flee from Your presence? If I ascend into heaven, You are there; If I make my bed in hell, behold, You are there. If I take the wings of the morning, And dwell in the uttermost parts of the sea, Even there Your hand shall lead me, And Your right hand shall hold me.
>
> Psalm 139:7–10

The Psalmist asks "Where?" and the answer comes: "You are there." It is not merely the thought of God that is "there," nor is it simply His influence, as some might conclude. He is a real Person, and *He is there.* This is the mystery of all mysteries—the presence and existence of God. How can He be everywhere at once and still be a real Person as we are? Our finite minds are controlled by a three-dimensional world (which the presence of God permeates) that limits our ability to conceive of things apart from bodies, buildings, places, objects, and so on.

A Definition of Omnipresence

Obviously, it is not easy to define the omnipresence of God. We are limited by our human bodies, and trying to comprehend how someone could be everywhere at once is not easy!

There are at least three essential parts of the definition of God's omnipresence, each of them equally important to our understanding.

1. God is in the universe, everywhere present at the same time. Job 22:12 says, "Is not God in the height of heaven? And see the highest stars, how lofty they are!" That text argues that God is present in the place of the "highest stars."

One of the best examples of God's presence being everywhere at the same time is found in Isaiah:

For thus says the High and Lofty One Who inhabits eternity, whose name is Holy: "I dwell in the high and holy place, With him who has a contrite and humble spirit, To revive the spirit of the humble, And to revive the heart of the contrite ones."

Isaiah 57:15

God says that He dwells in a *high and holy place,* but He also dwells with a *contrite and humble spirit.* One of our Christian songs asks the question "How Big Is God?" and the answer is that "He's big enough to rule His mighty universe, yet small enough to live within my heart." God indwells the bodies of believers, according to 1 Corinthians 6:19, but He is also dwelling at the "highest stars."

It is clear from Psalm 139:7–10 (quoted above) that God's presence is in heaven and hell (the grave) at the same time. There is no place we can go to escape His presence. When our daughter came up missing one Sunday after church, it was comforting to know that she was not away from the presence of God. She and a friend had decided to walk to the store, but they got lost by going in the wrong direction. When we could not find her, we finally called the police. They located her and her friend about five miles from our church. Needless to say, we had a few anxious moments, yet we were reminded of the importance of God's presence, watching over her.

2. The universe and all that it contains is in God. In Acts 17, Paul is preaching in Athens about God. He says:

"So that they should seek the Lord, in the hope that they might grope for Him and find Him, though He is not far from each one of us; for in Him we live and move and have our being, as also some of your own poets have said, 'For we are also His offspring.' "

Acts 17:27–28

That text says that "in Him we live and move and have our being." His presence includes all the material and physical universe which He has created, including mankind. As far as you could travel into space—and even beyond that—there is God's presence. All the planets and stars are within His omnipresence. In speaking of the earth, God says to Job:

> "Where were you when I laid the earth's foundations? Tell me, if you understand who marked off its dimensions? Surely you know! Who stretched a measuring line across it? On what were its footings set, or who laid its cornerstone?"
>
> Job 38:4–6, NIV

God "determined" the measurements of the earth. The earth is within the presence of God and its limitations are determined by Him. In verse 19 of that same chapter, God asks Job, "Where is the way to the dwelling of light? And darkness, where is its place?" In verse 24, He adds, "By what way is light diffused, Or the east wind scattered over the earth?" God then moves into the heavens and asks:

> "Can you bind the cluster of the Pleiades, Or loose the belt of Orion? Can you bring out Mazzaroth in its season? Or can you guide the Great Bear with its cubs? Do you know the ordinances of the heavens? Can you set their dominion over the earth?"
>
> Job 38:31–33

What incredible statements! God's presence is everywhere. The universe, including the constellations of stars, are within the scope of His presence and being constantly managed by Him.

Last night we were visiting friends in San Diego, California. Their home sits on top of a mountain. The sky was so clear, and the stars were out in full force. What a sight! We were all enjoying the view when we began sharing about the greatness of God. We realized that all the stars we were admiring were within the majestic presence of God. That thought alone was rather overwhelming in the light of that beautiful sight. My friend shared, "Just think—that great God is also living in our bodies." Were it not for clear biblical teaching about God's presence in the believer, it was almost too incredible to believe!

3. *God is separate from the universe in which He dwells.* Pantheism teaches that God is literally in everything. He is to be identified with the material universe. That is not taught in the Bible. In fact, the Bible makes it quite clear that God is separate from everything which He has made.

Psalm 99:1–3 emphasizes the Lord's separateness (holiness) from all which He created. In verse one we read,. "He dwells between the cherubim; Let the earth be moved!" In verse two is added: "He is high above all the peoples."

In 1 Kings 19, Elijah is running away from Jezebel and goes to a cave and hides there. The Lord speaks to him and asks, "What are you doing here, Elijah?" The Lord invites him to view a display of nature's power, but reminds him of an important truth: The Lord is greater than the power of nature. Verse 11 speaks of a "great and strong wind" which was breaking the rocks in pieces, but "the LORD was not in the wind." Then came an earthquake and these words, "But the LORD was not in the earthquake." Next came a fire and these words, "But the LORD was not in the fire." The point is that God is not to be identified with even the forces of nature. Nature is not God! God is above nature and uses it to accomplish His purposes: "Fire and hail, snow and clouds; Stormy wind, fulfilling His word" (Psalm 148:8).

Paul said to the philosophers of Athens:

> "The God who made the world and everything in it is the Lord of heaven and earth and does not live in temples built by hands. And he is not served by human hands, as if he needed anything, because he himself gives all men life and breath and everything else."
>
> Acts 17:24–25, NIV

God does not dwell in the bricks and stones. He is not in a table or a chair. His presence is separate from the material universe which He created. All material things exist within the omnipresence of God, but He remains separate from them.

So where is God? He is everywhere. His presence fills the whole universe (Jeremiah 23:24). Also, the material and physical universe is found within His presence, even though He is separate from it.

For us to think that God is not near is simply a denial of biblical truth. There is no place in this universe where we could go and not be in His presence. It is impossible for us to hide from God. Adam and Eve could not do it (Genesis 3:8–9), and neither can we. Hebrews 4:13 reminds us: "And there is no creature hidden from His sight, but all things are naked and open to the eyes of Him to whom we must give account."

But How Do We Explain . . . ?

To believe that God is omnipresent presents some problems to thinking people. There are at least three major difficulties that people encounter when trying to understand the Bible's teaching about the presence of God.

1. If God is everywhere, how can He be confined to one location such as heaven? Psalm 11:4 says, "The LORD is in His holy temple, The Lord's throne is in heaven; His eyes behold, His eyelids test the sons of men." Even though God is in heaven, He sees and is aware of the sons of men. In Psalm 14:2, we read: "The LORD looks down from heaven upon the children of men, To see if there are any who understand, who seek God." In 1 Kings 8:30, heaven is described as the dwelling place of God: "And may You hear the supplication of Your servant and of Your people Israel. When they pray toward this place, then hear in heaven Your dwelling place; and when You hear, forgive."

If He is in heaven, how can He be everywhere at once? The answer that seems most plausible is that God is not everywhere present in the same sense. He is able to manifest Himself in special ways in different places. His presence in one place is not the same as His presence in another place, although we are not told what that difference is.

God is able to localize His presence by special revelation or visible evidence. He appeared in the pillar of fire by night and the cloud by day when He led the children of Israel through the wilderness. He appeared to Moses in the burning bush, and His special presence was represented by smoke filling the temple in the days of Isaiah. Not one of these figures (fire, cloud, smoke, burning bush) tells us all there is to know about the presence of God. They were simply visible manifestations of His presence. All of that which is His presence was not seen in any one of these symbols. Only a part of what is true about His presence is visible and known.

2. If God is everywhere, how can anyone "flee" from His presence? On several occasions we read of someone who is fleeing the presence of God. If He is everywhere at once, is not that an impossibility? The answer to that is both "yes" and "no." Naturally, we cannot hide or run away from God's presence and knowledge. However, from man's point of view, there is a sense in which we are doing the "running." We depart from conscious fellowship with Him.

In Job 1:12, we read: "So the LORD said to Satan, 'Behold, all that he has is in your power, only do not lay a hand on his person.' Then Satan went out from the presence of the LORD." God's presence in this case is localized in heaven. He, no doubt, gives a visible manifestation of Himself. Satan leaves that visible manifestation of God's presence in heaven, even though there is no place where Satan can go that will escape the presence of God. Job 2:7 adds: "Then Satan went out from the presence of the LORD." We are told in verse one that Satan came along with the "sons of God [angels]" to present himself "before the LORD." Once again we assume a visible manifestation of God—sitting upon His throne in heaven. It is that special presence from which Satan departs.

In Jonah 1:10 we read this statement: "For the men knew that he fled from the presence of the LORD, because he had told them." This refers to Jonah's trying to run away from God. Of course, that is an impossibility in one sense—God is everywhere. However, Jonah is running away from the conscious presence of the Lord, which he as a finite being had experienced. Verse three tells us that

Jonah was fleeing from the presence of the Lord after hearing God's message to him about going to Nineveh.

One other example is that of Cain: "Then Cain went out from the presence of the LORD, and dwelt in the land of Nod, on the east of Eden" (Genesis 4:16). The Lord's presence was localized and manifested in a special sense in the Garden of Eden. Back in Genesis 3:8, we read: "And they heard the sound of the LORD God walking in the garden in the cool of the day, and Adam and his wife hid themselves from the presence of the LORD God among the trees of the garden." God seemed close by, and they thought they could hide from Him. Of course, they could not. But this passage, along with the one about Cain, illustrates how God's presence was manifested in a special way in the Garden of Eden. It is clear that Adam and Eve could not hide from the presence of God, nor can we. He is everywhere, but He can also limit the manifestation of His presence (as far as man is concerned) whenever He chooses to do so.

3. If God is everywhere, how could He dwell in a physical body? This is a serious issue as it relates to the identity of Jesus Christ. Is God able to localize Himself in a physical body, and still be everywhere at once? If He can give special manifestations of His presence in a given place (such as heaven or the Garden of Eden, and so on), could He not also do the same in a physical body? This seems like a more difficult question, but it also seems possible.

Colossians 1:19 says, "For it pleased the Father that in Him [Jesus Christ] all the fullness should dwell." The term *all the fullness* seems to express the totality of God's Person and attributes, and according to this verse, that totality dwells in Jesus Christ. That this refers to the physical body of Jesus Christ is clear from Colossians 2:9: "For in Him [Jesus Christ] dwells all the fullness of the Godhead bodily." This is a remarkable statement! Jesus Christ is God manifest in the flesh: "And without controversy great is the mystery of godliness: God was manifested in the flesh, Justified in the Spirit, Seen by angels, Preached among the

Gentiles, Believed on in the world, Received up in glory" (1 Timothy 3:16). The Apostle John says of Jesus Christ in John 1:14: "And the Word became flesh, and dwelt among us, and we beheld His glory, the glory as of the only begotten of the Father, full of grace and truth." John 1:1 says that "the Word was God."

God's omnipresence was localized in the Person and body of Jesus Christ. He was not part of God, but all God! He was both God and man at the same time. Philippians 2:6 puts it this way: "Who [Jesus Christ], being in the form of God, did not consider it robbery to be equal with God." The word *form* refers to the exact essence or nature of something. Jesus was and is God! "This is the true God and eternal life" (1 John 5:20).

It is a mystery how God, who is omnipresent, could localize Himself at all, whether in Old Testament manifestations, or in the Person of Jesus Christ. But the fact remains—He did it! As God, His abilities are far greater than our ability to understand.

Why Is God's Presence So Comforting?

To those who believe in Him, God's presence is the strength of their lives. God is there at all times to minister to us in our need. He cares and invites us to trust Him. Proverbs 3:5–6 says: "Trust in the LORD with all your heart, And lean not on your own understanding; In all your ways acknowledge Him, And He shall direct your paths." Consider the marvelous blessings that arise from the fact of God's existence and presence.

1. God's presence gives stability. "I have set the LORD always before me; Because *He is at my right hand* I shall not be moved" (Psalm 16:8).

We live in a world of change where nothing seems to remain constant. The circumstances of life cause us to be insecure and unstable. We do not know from one day to the next what is going to happen. But the Lord's presence is the stabilizing factor: "The eternal God is your refuge, And *underneath are the everlasting arms*" (Deuteronomy 33:27). What security! What stability! Malachi 3:6 reminds us, "For I am the LORD, I do not change. . . ."

James 1:17 adds: "Every good and every perfect gift is from above, and comes down from the Father of lights, with whom there is no variation or shadow of turning."

Although change can at times be very threatening, there is the One who does not change. Our Lord can be trusted to bring stability to us when we feel so insecure. He is there, as David said, "at my right hand."

Those words were greatly used to bring stability to a friend's heart when he learned that he had lost his job. He had worked for this company for over thirty years, and being laid off was a tremendous shock to his system. His great encouragement came from the assurance of God's presence, which does bring stability when we feel insecure.

2. *God's presence eliminates fear of dying.* "Yea, though I walk through the valley of the shadow of death, I will fear no evil; *For You are with me*; Your rod and Your staff, they comfort me" (Psalm 23:4).

The prospect of death never seems so real as that moment we are told by our physician that we have a terminal illness. I remember how frightened was the woman who called me on the phone one day. She was forty-two years old and full of life, but her doctor had just informed her that she had cancer and had only about six months to live. She was scared and was crying uncontrollably. At a time like that, we need assurance that God is there and will be with us through the pain and tears. In the months ahead, her illness worsened, and she was finally hospitalized, never to return to her home and family. In the closing days before she died, her greatest joy was repeating Psalm 23:4 to herself—"I will fear no evil; *For You are with me*." In discovering the comfort of God's presence, she became a blessing because of it to all who visited her in those closing, agonizing days of her life on earth. She is now in the presence of the Lord Himself, as we are assured:

> Therefore we are always confident, knowing that while we are at home in the body we are absent from the Lord. For we walk by faith, not by sight. We are confident, yes, well

pleased rather to be absent from the body and *to be present with the Lord.*

2 Corinthians 5:6–8

3. God's presence offers protection in times of crisis and difficulty.

But now, thus says the Lord, who created you, O Jacob, and He Who formed you, O Israel: "Fear not, for I have redeemed you; I have called you by your name; You are Mine. When you pass through the waters, *I will be with you*; And through the rivers, they shall not overflow you. When you walk through the fire, you shall not be burned, Nor shall the flame scorch you."

Isaiah 43:1–2

Later, in verse five, the Lord speaks to His people and says, "Fear not, for I am with you." The assurance of God's presence gives us great comfort in times of trial and crisis. Psalm 125:2 adds a beautiful thought: "As the mountains surround Jerusalem, So the LORD surrounds His people From this time forth and forever."

God took care of Israel in her many hours of trial and suffering. He never left their side. His presence was always there, surrounding them and protecting them: "For He shall stand *at the right hand* of the poor, to save him from those who condemn him" (Psalm 109:31).

4. God's presence encourages us in prayer. We all have times when we pray and wonder if God is there. Does He hear us when we call? Psalm 145:18 states: "*The LORD is near* to all who call upon Him, To all who call upon Him in truth." In Isaiah 55:6, we read, "Seek the LORD while He may be found, Call upon Him while *He is near.*"

It is especially true in times of tears that the Lord's presence is comforting when we pray. Psalm 34:18 puts it like this: "*The Lord is near* to those who have a broken heart, And saves such as have a contrite spirit." Psalm 73:28 says, "But it is good for me to draw *near to God.* . . ." James 4:8 adds: "Draw near to God and *He will draw near to you.* . . ."

Our prayer life becomes much more meaningful when we know of the nearness of God. He is there, listening and caring.

5. *It produces courage.* Moses told Joshua (Deuteronomy 31:8) about his role as leader of the children of Israel: "And the LORD, He is the One who goes before you. *He will be with you,* He will not leave you nor forsake you; do not fear nor be dismayed."

The Lord repeated that to Joshua directly: "Have not I commanded you? Be strong and of good courage; do not be afraid, nor be dismayed, for *the Lord your God is with you* wherever you go" (Joshua 1:9).

Jesus told us similar words in Matthew 28:20: ". . . and lo, *I am with you always,* even to the end of the age." Hebrews 13:5 quotes the Lord's words to Joshua and applies them to us today: "I will never leave you nor forsake you." What wonderful assurance!

There are many problems in life we must face with courage and resolve. There are times of confrontation which cause most of us to back off and avoid conflict. Courage arises when we are confident of the Lord's will and presence.

God's existence and presence with us bring tremendous comfort. To know that He is there—at your right hand—will help you in a difficult trial or time of sorrow. It will encourage you to pray to Him often, trusting Him to lead, protect, and give you courage to face what must inevitably come to all of us.

Stephen Charnock has a great comment on the comfort of God's presence:

> It is not a piece of God is here and another parcel there, but God in His whole essence and perfections; in His wisdom to guide us, His power to protect and support us, His mercy to pity us, His fulness to refresh us, and His goodness to relieve us: He is ready to sparkle out in this or that perfection, as the necessities of His people require, and His own wisdom directs for His own honor; so that being not far from us in an excellency of His nature, we can quickly have recourse to Him upon any emergency; so that if we are miserable, we have the presence of His goodness; if we want direction, we have the presence of His wisdom; if we are weak, we have the presence of His power, and should we not rejoice in it, as

a man doth in the presence of a powerful, wealthy, and compassionate friend?*

Questions to Ponder

1. What do we mean by the omnipresence of God?
2. Is God dwelling in material things, such as a table?
3. If God is everywhere, how can He be confined to one location, such as heaven?
4. How can anyone flee the presence of God if He is everywhere?
5. How could God dwell in a physical body if He is everywhere?
6. What blessings does the knowledge of God's omnipresence bring to the believer?

---

* *Discourses Upon the Existence and Attributes of God, Vol. 1.* (Grand Rapids: Baker Book House, reprinted in 1979 from the 1853 edition of Robert Carter and Brothers), p. 402.

7

How Powerful Is God?

What can God do? One of the interesting things about people's understanding of God is how often they relate His power to the subject of physical healing. In the July 4, 1983, issue of *Time* magazine, a report on faith healing is given in the "Religion" section. The reporter penned these remarks: "It was impossible to discern which people might have been cured and which were subject only to passing psychological relief."

After a racquetball game, I went to the steam room to relax and try to lose some more weight. Several men filled that little room, and one man was telling his story about how God had recently healed his back. I became quite interested in his story as he began speaking eloquently of the mighty power of God. I asked him how his back was feeling now. He replied that it still hurt a little, but it was much better. I said, "It doesn't look as if God did a very good job!" He snapped back, "What are you, an unbeliever?" I said, "No, but I do wonder why God couldn't take all your soreness away if He really healed you." The man replied, "God is powerful, but He can't do everything, you know!"

That kind of rationalizing, an attempt to explain apparent weaknesses in the healing ability of God, just does not convince me. If the God of the Bible healed him, there would be no question about it! Most people are unaware of what the Bible really teaches about the power of God. They spend a lot of time trying to defend His apparent lack of concern, what seems to be (from their point of

111

view) certain limitations of God. If He can do anything and everything, why does He not? Perhaps He is not as powerful as we think!
Maybe the problem is our faith. It did not happen—because we did
not believe enough in His power. That is what many people who
pray for healing, but do not experience it, are told by certain faith
healers—"You didn't have enough faith, or you would have been
healed."

Is God powerful enough to heal you? Can He put your marriage
back together? Can He give you a better job? Could He give you
more money? How about a new car? Can He stop nations from
going to war against each other? Can He stop a storm or earthquake
from happening in your community? Can He keep you from getting old? Can He cure cancer?

One of the most serious criminal problems in this country is the
kidnapping of children and young people. I remember the couple
whose only child was picked up one day by the wife's former
husband. Two friends saw it happen, but assumed that nothing was
wrong. The couple went through two horrible years of grief and
emotional heartache, waiting for some news of what had happened
to their child. The wife asked me one day, "Is God powerful
enough to bring my child back to me?" Much prayer was offered
in behalf of this family. Finally, the police discovered where the
child was and apprehended the former husband who had taken the
boy away from his mother and stepfather. This story had a happy
ending, but others do not. How powerful is God in a situation like
this? What does the Bible teach about the power of God?

A Biblical Definition

God is referred to as the all-powerful or Almighty God in the
Bible. Revelation 19:6 (used in Handel's *Messiah*) tells us that
"the Lord God Omnipotent reigns!" *Omnipotence* is the word
theologians use to refer to God's power. It means He has all
power. God is frequently called "the Almighty" when referring to
His works or His judgments. In describing His presence in the

eternal state, Revelation calls Him "Lord God Almighty" (Revelation 21:22).

The residents of heaven sing praises to God continually, and they call Him "Lord God Almighty" (Revelation 4:8; 11:17; 15:3). God refers to Himself as "Almighty God" when He appears to Abraham and announces His covenant with him (Genesis 17:1–2). The New Testament word for "Almighty" (*pantokrator*) appears ten times, and the Old Testament word (*Shadday*), forty-eight times.

In putting together a definition of God's power from the biblical information we have, we discover at least four concepts in that definition. Each contributes to our understanding and will help us answer the question "How powerful is God?"

God Can Do All Things!

The Bible frequently affirms this truth, and usually does not try to answer all of the difficulties which such a statement can cause to our finite minds. For example, Job's reply to God's evaluation of his situation is: "I know that *You can do everything,* And that no purpose of Yours can be withheld from You" (Job 42:2). While this declaration asserts the ability of God, it also suggests that God does what He wants to do—His purpose controls His power. The question is not so much "*Can* He do it?" but "*Will* He do it?"

Jesus Christ gives this clear teaching about God's power when He answers the disciples' question about who can be saved if it is so hard for a rich man to enter the kingdom of heaven: "With men this is impossible, but with God *all things are possible*" (Matthew 19:26). Once again we are given the clue that while God's power can do all things in that they are "possible," it does not automatically mean that He will do it.

A little boy about six years old fell down and scraped his knee right in front of me. He was running on the sidewalk of the church's educational building and was not looking at all the hazards of the ground below him. He was crying, and I immediately went over and picked him up. I took his handkerchief and carefully wiped the dirt and blood off his knee. He looked up and asked, "Can God make the sore go away?" This was no time for a theological discourse, but I said, "He sure can, but He may want the sore to stay for a little while so you can remember why it happened and not do it again." The boy seemed happy with that, and off he went.

We state emphatically what the Bible teaches, that God can do anything and everything, but we add: Everything that He *wants* to do.

Nothing Is Too Hard for God to Do!

An additional thought is necessary to the concept that God can do all things: There is nothing too hard or difficult for Him to do if He wants to do it.

A great story on this point is found in the book of Genesis, concerning Abraham and Sarah. Consider these verses:

> And He said, "I will certainly return to you according to the time of life, and behold, Sarah your wife shall have a son." And Sarah was listening in the tent door which was behind him. Now Abraham and Sarah were old, well-advanced in age; and Sarah had passed the age of childbearing. Therefore Sarah laughed within herself, saying, "After I have grown old, shall I have pleasure, my lord being old also?" And the LORD said to Abraham, "Why did Sarah laugh, saying, 'Shall I surely bear a child, since I am old?' Is anything too hard for the LORD? At the appointed time I will return to you, according to the time of life, and Sarah shall have a son." But Sarah denied it, saying, "I did not laugh," for she was afraid. And He said, "No, but you did laugh!"
>
> Genesis 18:10–15

Do not criticize Sarah! You would have laughed too, if God told you at age eighty-nine that you would have a baby next year! God called the name of the boy, Isaac, which in Hebrew means "laughter." He was a constant reminder of the great power of God, and they would laugh with joy: "Is anything too hard for the Lord?"

This story answers, "Of course not!" If He wants to do it, He *can* do it!

Jeremiah's prayer reminds us that there is nothing too hard for God to do: "Ah, LORD GOD! Behold, You have made the heavens and the earth by Your great power and outstretched arm. *There is nothing too hard for You*" (Jeremiah 32:17).

A best-selling book by Rabbi Harold Kushner, *When Bad Things Happen to Good People,* comes to a different conclusion. The author reasons through the Book of Job and concludes that God is limited—there are some things He cannot do. Although this conflicts with the teachings of the Bible, the author prefers it to the alternatives available. Assuming that the reluctance of God to do something, especially to stop evil from happening, indicates His lack of concern, the author chooses to believe that God is limited—rather than believe that He does not care. Neither of these is the right answer, according to the Scriptures. God cares, and He can do anything He wants to do. Obviously, there are things He chooses not to do. His greater knowledge and purpose control His acts of power and love.

God Will Do What Is Consistent with His Nature, Character, and Purposes!

At this point we begin to understand some reasons why God does or does not do certain things. When people ask, "Can God make a rock that He cannot move?" they reveal their misunderstanding of who God is and what He does do. Such a decision by God would be inconsistent for Him to do. These reasonings are an insult to God, whose lovely character and mighty power will not stoop to such foolishness. There are many things that God simply will not do.

When Jesus was tempted by the devil in the wilderness, the devil tried to get Him to display His power and satisfy His need of hunger (Matthew 4:1–11). "If You are the Son of God, command that these stones become bread" (verse 3).

Jesus answered: "Man shall not live by bread alone, but by every word that proceeds from the mouth of God" (verse 4).

Taking Jesus up to Jerusalem and setting Him on the pinnacle (where two walls meet) of the temple, the devil said: "If you are the Son of God, throw yourself down" (verse 6). He then quoted from Psalm 91 about the protection the angels would give if He did such a thing.

Jesus answered: "You shall not tempt the LORD your God" (verse 7).

It is evident that there are things the Lord will not do. They are contrary to His purposes. It is not a question of "Can He?" but "Will He?"—and even "Should He?"

Some of the things that God *will not* do or even *cannot* do include:

1. God cannot lie.

Paul wrote to Titus:

> Paul, a servant of God and an apostle of Jesus Christ, according to the faith of God's elect and the acknowledgement of the truth which is according to godliness, in hope of eternal life which God, *who cannot lie,* promised before time began, but has in due time manifested His word through preaching, which was committed to me according to the commandment of God our Savior.
>
> Titus 1:1–3

Eternal life was promised to us by God, who cannot lie. That hope is resting on the veracity and trustworthiness of God Himself. Imagine the implications if God lied even once! How could He be trusted?

2. God cannot be tempted by evil, nor does He tempt anyone else to do evil.

> Let no one say when he is tempted, "I am tempted by God"; for God *cannot be tempted by evil, nor does He Himself tempt anyone.*
>
> James 1:13

This particular point is so important to our understanding of temptation and why it happens. We typically will blame anyone or anything (including God) for the temptations we experience—especially when we yield to them. God cannot be blamed, for He simply will not tempt anyone to do wrong. That is inconsistent with His character and purposes.

A young man came to my office one day to talk about a personal matter. When he arrived, he was quite nervous and had a difficult time explaining himself. It seems he had committed sexual immorality several times and was deeply convicted about it. In the process of our conversation, he began to justify his actions on the basis of his environment and the devil's temptations. He even made that classic remark "the devil made me do it!" As we cleared that matter up, he began to think that maybe God was behind all of this, so he argued, "If God didn't want me to sin, He could have stopped me." But God does not do that. Each of us sins because we want to do it (James 1:13–15). Plain and simple—you did it because you wanted to do it! There is no one to blame but yourself! God never tempts anyone to do evil.

3. God cannot deny Himself.

> If we are faithless, He remains faithful; He cannot deny Himself.
>
> 2 Timothy 2:13

God will not go back on His promises nor deny His own character in being faithful to what He has said. We are often "faithless" and unreliable because we are human. God is always faithful to what He has said. Therefore, when given the chance, God will never deny Himself—He simply cannot and will not do anything that is inconsistent with His nature and purposes.

God Is Never Exhausted by the Exercise of His Power!

The fourth part of our definition of God is often assumed, but needs to be declared frequently. No matter how strong anyone of us is, he or she will get tired by the continual exercise of strength. God never does. He has an inexhaustible supply.

> Have you not known? Have you not heard? The everlasting God, the LORD, the Creator of the ends of the earth, Neither faints nor is weary. There is no searching of His understanding. He gives power to the weak, And to those who have no might He increases strength. Even the youths shall faint and be weary, And the young men shall utterly fall, But those who wait on the LORD shall renew their strength; They shall mount up with wings like eagles, They shall run and not be weary, They shall walk and not faint.
>
> Isaiah 40:28–31

That text says it so clearly and vividly: *The Creator neither faints nor is weary.* It tells us that even strong young men will be faint and weary, and sometimes fall. If you are middle-aged or over, that brings joy to your heart!

I once watched a young man in the weight room of our athletic club put on an amazing display of power and stamina. His strength was hard to believe, and he kept doing exercises and lifts at a record-setting pace. After some time elapsed, I noticed a sign of fatigue showing as his pace became slower. I thought to myself, "He's strong all right, but not as strong as my God! He's already getting tired, and my God never does!" I'm not real sure what that thought did to me, but it relieved me of the pressure of trying to compete with that young man. If I would have tried, I would have gone home to be with my God! He never gets tired, but I surely do.

Not only does God never get tired in the exercise of His power, He never needs to sleep either. The Psalmist speaks of the importance of this truth:

> I will lift up my eyes to the hills—From whence comes my help? My help comes from the LORD, Who made heaven and earth. He will not allow your foot to be moved; He who keeps you will not slumber. Behold, He who keeps Israel Shall neither slumber nor sleep. The LORD is your keeper; The LORD is your shade at your right hand. The sun shall not

strike you by day, Nor the moon by night. The LORD shall preserve you from all evil; He shall preserve your soul. The LORD shall preserve your going out and your coming in From this time forth, and even forevermore.

Psalm 121:1–8

In attempting to define the omnipotence of God, we have shared at least four concepts:

- God can do all things.
- Nothing is too hard for God to do.
- God will do that which is consistent with His nature, character, and purposes.
- God is never exhausted by the exercise of His power.

Definitions are good, but the impact of those definitions is best felt when we see the actual display of God's power. Just what kind of things does God do which prove what our definition has told us?

Evidences of God's Power

People want proof. You cannot just tell them—you must show them. God realizes that more than we do, and He has often revealed His mighty power to people on earth. He has shown us that His power is behind all of what we see in the material universe, as well as in the processes of natural law. He has frequently interrupted the natural and performed the supernatural.

Creation of the Universe

For since the creation of the world His invisible attributes are clearly seen, being understood by the things that are made, even His eternal *power* and Godhead, so that they are without excuse.

Romans 1:20

With one look at the created universe one quickly understands something of the mighty power of God—it is awesome! Words are inadequate to describe such power. To try to explain its presence by natural law is hopeless. The telescopic and microscopic worlds are wonders to behold and are clear testimony to the enormous power and genius of the Creator. Bible writers attest to this fact on many occasions, as did the Prophet Jeremiah: "He has made the earth by His power" (Jeremiah 10:12).

Psalm 8:3 speaks of the heavens, the moon, and the stars as "the work of Your [God's] fingers." It was just finger-play! Psalm 19:1 adds that "the heavens declare the glory of God; And the firmament shows His handiwork." The evidence of God's mighty power is there if we want to see it! Psalm 102:25 says of God, "And the heavens are the work of Your hands."

The Processes of Nature

Jeremiah tells us that God's power is working in the process of evaporation, rain, lightning, and wind:

> "When He utters His voice, there is a multitude of waters in the heavens; and He causes the vapors to ascend from the ends of the earth. He makes lightning for the rain, He brings the wind out of His treasuries."
>
> Jeremiah 10:13

The Psalmist says:

> He sends the springs into the valleys, Which flow among the hills. . . . He causes the grass to grow for the cattle, And vegetation for the service of man, That He may bring forth food from the earth.
>
> Psalm 104:10, 14

We are also told that the fish of the sea are fed by God and that their very life depends upon God (verses 25–29). One of the great statements about God's involvement in the processes of nature is in verse 30: "You renew the face of the earth."

The Laws of the Universe

Why do the planets not collide? Why do objects fall to the earth and not out into space? We know that certain laws operate behind the scenes to keep the universe functioning properly. The Bible teaches that God is manifesting His power in these laws, which we have all learned to accept as facts.

Colossians 1:17 says concerning God the Son, "And He is before all things, and in Him all things consist [hold together]." Hebrews 1:3 adds, ". . . upholding all things by the word of His power." God's power is sustaining all the physical laws of the universe. You may not agree that God is the One doing it, but something or Someone is! God inquires of Job: "Do you know the ordinances [laws] of the heavens? Can you set their dominion over the earth?" (Job 38:33).

God spoke to Job about His power in the laws of the universe in order to challenge Job to trust Him completely in the times of suffering which he had endured:

> "Where were you when I laid the foundations of the earth? Tell Me, if you have understanding. Who determined its measurements? Surely you know! Or who stretched the line upon it? To what were the foundations fastened? Or who laid its cornerstone, When the morning stars sang together, And all the sons of God shouted for joy?"
>
> Job 38:4–7

The Plagues of Egypt

One of the great displays of the power of God happened in Egypt over 3,000 years ago. When you visit Egypt today, you are constantly confronted with the story of Israel's presence there. They still remember. While many question the validity of what happened, or we might say the extent to which events described in the Bible really occurred, everyone agrees that something unusual did indeed happen. Many of us are convinced that amazing miracles and demonstrations of God's power actually took place.

The entire history of the Old Testament is filled with continual reminders and admonitions of how God redeemed Israel out of Egypt. In the Book of Deuteronomy (the Second Law—given by Moses on the east side of the Jordan River just before Israel entered its land), fathers are told to instruct their children about what happened in Egypt:

> "Then you shall say to your son: 'We were slaves of Pharaoh in Egypt, and the LORD brought us out of Egypt with a mighty hand; and the LORD showed signs and wonders before our eyes, great and severe, against Egypt, Pharaoh, and all his household.' "
>
> Deuteronomy 6:21–22

These signs and wonders included ten plagues. The magicians of Pharaoh were able to counterfeit the first two plagues (waters turned into blood and an infestation of frogs), according to Exodus 7:22 and 8:7, but when the third plague (lice) hit, they could not duplicate it and said to Pharaoh: "This is the finger of God" (Exodus 8:19). They began to realize the awesome power of God.

The interesting thing about this Egyptian encounter with the power of God is that it was predicted by God before it occurred. In Exodus 7:3, God said to Moses, "And I will harden Pharaoh's heart, and multiply My signs and My wonders in the land of Egypt." According to Exodus 9:16, God did all of this to show His power to all the earth.

After Israel crossed the Red Sea through another display of God's mighty power, God destroyed Pharaoh and his army in the sea. Moses wrote this song of victory to the Lord:

> "Your right hand, O Lord, has become glorious in power;
> Your right hand, O Lord, has dashed the enemy in pieces.
> And in the greatness of Your excellence You have over-

thrown those who rose against You; You sent forth Your wrath which consumed them like stubble. And with the blast of Your nostrils The waters were gathered together; The floods stood upright like a heap; And the depths congealed in the heart of the sea. The enemy said, 'I will pursue, I will overtake, I will divide the spoil; My desire shall be satisfied on them. I will draw my sword, My hand shall destroy them.' You blew with Your wind, The sea covered them; They sank like lead in the mighty waters. Who is like You, O Lord, among the gods? Who is like You, glorious in holiness, Fearful in praises, doing wonders? You stretched out Your right hand; The earth swallowed them. You in Your mercy have led forth the people whom You have redeemed; You have guided them in Your strength To Your holy habitation.''

Exodus 15:6–13

The Miracles of Jesus Christ

It was well reported in the first century A.D. that a man in Israel was able to perform miracles. He could heal the sick, calm a stormy sea, feed 5,000 people with one boy's lunch, walk on water, and even raise the dead! Josephus, the Jewish historian, mentions Jesus in his historical account of the Jewish battle with Rome. In *Antiquities of the Jews,* chapter 3, he writes:

Now there was about this time Jesus, a wise man, if it be lawful to call him a man; for he was a doer of wonderful works, a teacher of such men as receive the truth with pleasure. He drew over to him both many of the Jews and many of the Gentiles. He was the Christ. And when Pilate, at the suggestion of the principal men amongst us, had condemned him to the cross, those that loved him at the first did not forsake him; for he appeared to them alive again the third day; as the divine prophets had foretold these and ten thousand other wonderful things concerning him. And the tribe of Christians, so named from him, are not extinct at this day.

The New Testament says of Jesus:

> And there are also many other things that Jesus did, which if
> they were written one by one, I suppose that even the world
> itself could not contain the books that would be written.
>
> John 21:25

The Gospel of John also tells us about the purpose of the miracles:

> And truly Jesus did many other signs in the presence of His
> disciples, which are not written in this book; but these are
> written that you may believe that Jesus is the Christ, the Son
> of God, and that believing you may have life in His name.
>
> John 20:30, 31

On the Day of Pentecost, Simon Peter spoke of the miraculous abilities of Jesus Christ:

> "Jesus of Nazareth, a Man attested by God to you by miracles, wonders, and signs which God did through Him in your
> midst, as you yourselves also know."
>
> Acts 2:22

Although miracles are a demonstration of God's power (if they clearly are supernatural), they do not always convince people. Though many saw His miracles performed, they still did not believe His claims. Perhaps He was a magician, or worse yet, an instrument of satanic power. These miracles were evidence of His claim to be the Messiah. We might call them His credentials. Isaiah speaks of what God will do to display His power: "Then the eyes of the blind shall be opened, And the ears of the deaf shall be unstopped. Then the lame shall leap like a deer, And the tongue of the dumb sing" (Isaiah 35:5–6).

The Resurrection of Jesus Christ

Talk about power! Ephesians 1:19–20 wants us to know . . . "What is the exceeding greatness of His *power* toward us who believe, according to the working of His *mighty power* which He worked in Christ when He raised Him from the dead.''

Jesus said:

> "No one takes it [My life] from Me, but I lay it down of Myself. I have *power* to lay it down, and I have *power* to take it again. . . .''
>
> John 10:18

Romans 1:4 states: "And declared to be the Son of God with *power,* according to the Spirit of holiness, by the resurrection from the dead.''

The Apostle Paul wrote in Philippians 3:10: "That I may know Him [Jesus] and the *power* of His resurrection." Christianity is built upon the historical fact that Jesus Christ rose from the dead. If He did not, true Christianity would collapse. To the believer, the resurrection is the great demonstration of God's power.

I was trying to comfort a young wife whose husband had been killed in an automobile accident, when she asked, "Pastor, did the resurrection really happen?" There was a seriousness and concern in her question that day which remains with me today. The only comfort that sustained her then is what sustains all true believers in Jesus Christ, and that is the hope of the resurrection. If God's power raised Jesus from the dead, then He is capable of raising all of us from the dead. It is as simple as that!

The evidences of God's power in the past should build our confidence in the power of God for the future. The Bible teaches that God's power will be displayed once again, as it was in Egypt over 3,000 years ago. This time it will affect the entire world, not just one country. There will occur catastrophic events whose only explanation will be the mighty power of God. The last book of the Bible, Revelation, records these events. Revelation 16:9 reveals that the people of earth will know that God is showing His power through these awful plagues—yet they will not repent and believe in Him. That is the tragedy of human nature. Our pride and self-ishness keep us from knowing and believing in the one and only God, the God of power.

Why We Need God's Power

Assuming we believe that God's power is real and available, why do we need it in our lives? That is somewhat like asking whether grass needs water to grow. It should be obvious that we need help of an extraordinary kind. In a narcissistic society, where people begin and end with themselves, the poverty of human solutions and pursuits becomes more evident with each passing year. Our powerlessness to change the moral decay and meaninglessness of our lives is all too apparent. We need help!

The man sitting in my office was the epitome of despair and disappointment. All of his life he was in charge (so he thought), but things never turned out the way he wanted. His marriage broke up, his children turned away from him and his values, his job was given to a younger man, and his ideals were destroyed before his eyes. He never needed anyone or anything until now. He thought he could manage effectively and produce consistently over the years of his life. Everything now seemed like a boy's fantasy. He asked me, "What do I do now?" When I suggested he needed God's help and power, he said, "What good will that do?" The following reasons are an attempt to answer that question.

Our Limitations

It is a shock to a man who has enjoyed athletic prowess and physical strength most of his life to discover his weakness. The old knees do not move as they once did. He gets out of breath before the game is over and his body aches more. He can't run as fast or as long, and his quickness is gone. Younger men give him that condescending smile that suggests he is too old and should maybe join the wheelchair crowd!

Isaiah speaks of our need for God's strength, simply because of our limitations:

> Have you not known? Have you not heard? The everlasting
> God, the LORD, The Creator of the ends of the earth, Neither

faints nor is weary. There is no searching of His understanding. He gives power to the weak, And to those who have no might He increases strength. Even the youths shall faint and be weary, And the young men shall utterly fall, But those who wait on the LORD shall renew their strength; They shall mount up with wings like eagles, They shall run and not be weary, They shall walk and not faint.

Isaiah 40:28–31

Note verse 29: "He gives *power* to the weak." Have you sensed your weakness lately? The Apostle Paul wrote:

And He said to me, "My grace is sufficient for you, for My strength is made perfect in weakness." Therefore most gladly I will rather boast in my infirmities, that the power of Christ may rest upon me. Therefore I take pleasure in infirmities, in reproaches, in needs, in persecutions, in distresses, for Christ's sake. For when I am weak, then I am strong.

2 Corinthians 12:9–10

When I am weak, then I am strong. God's strength and power are greatly needed in our weakness. It is something special to know His power when you are faced with your limitations.

Ephesians 3:20 says, "Now to Him who is able to do exceedingly abundantly above all that we ask or think, according to the *power* that works in us." His power can do more than we can ask or think. Strange that we do not call upon Him more! Our prideful "self-sufficiency" prevents that, until a few trying experiences of defeat point out our need. The need has been there all along, but our self-confident inability to admit weakness keeps us from depending upon God and His power. But: "I can do all things through Christ who strengthens me" (Philippians 4:13). Inward spiritual power is much greater than outward physical strength. Our limitations are reminders of our need for God's power.

Samson is one man who learned the secret of God's power—the hard way. (Read Judges 16.) His hair was an outward symbol of God's power, and when it was cut, his great strength was gone.

His enemies, the Philistines, made a great feast in the temple of their god to celebrate their apparent victory over Samson, who had defeated them on so many occasions. Samson was mocked in their presence. They had gouged out his eyes and chained him. Samson made one last appeal to God to display His power and destroy the Philistines. After asking a young boy to guide him toward the pillars of the temple, he called on the Lord and pushed those pillars down, and the entire structure collapsed, killing about 3,000 people, including Samson himself.

Our Salvation

We cannot save ourselves from sin, death, and hell. It takes the power of God. The gospel of Christ is called "the *power* of God to salvation for everyone who believes" (Romans 1:16).

It is the mystery of Christianity that requires a person to trust the power of God, rather than depend on human performance. One man said to me, "If it's free, I don't think it's worth having; and if I can't earn it, I don't want it." That was his reply to my description of the salvation which God offers to us—it must be believed, and it cannot be earned nor do we deserve it.

The disciples of Jesus were perplexed over His remarks about the difficulty rich men have in being converted. He said that it was easier for a camel to go through the eye of a needle than for a rich man to enter the kingdom of God (Matthew 19:2). Upon that remark, the disciples asked, "Who then can be saved?" Jesus replied, "With men this is impossible, but with God all things are possible" (verses 25–26). God's power is needed!

God's Promises

The power of God is needed to back up the promises of God. What assurance do we have that He can do what He claims if He does not have power or the ability to do them?

The Book of Romans tells us of Abraham's confidence in God's promise to him:

> He did not waver at the promise of God through unbelief, but was strengthened in faith, giving glory to God, and being fully convinced that what He had promised He was able to perform.
>
> Romans 4:20–21

Abraham's confidence had to be in the power of God in order for that promise to be fulfilled. When he was ninety-nine years old and impotent, and his wife at eighty-nine years was barren, God promised that they would have a son in one year. The only way that could happen is if a miracle was performed by the power of God. God's power is behind His promises.

In 1 Corinthians 6:14, we read, "And God both raised up the Lord and will also raise us up by His power." I believe in the promise of God to all believers that we will be raised from the dead to live forever with the Lord. My faith in that promise exists because I know and believe that God has the power to do it!

Our Security

I am convinced that the salvation I have by faith in Jesus Christ shall never be taken away from me. I base my confidence on the power of God, not my ability to perform. God's power keeps me: "Who are kept by the power of God through faith for salvation ready to be revealed in the last time" (1 Peter 1:5).

> For I am persuaded that neither death nor life, nor angels nor principalities nor powers, nor things present nor things to come, nor height nor depth, nor any other created thing, shall be able to separate us from the love of God which is in Christ Jesus our Lord.
>
> Romans 8:38–39

That is what I call security! What can separate us? Absolutely nothing! God's power to keep us prevents it.

A young girl shared with me her insecurity—she had great doubts about her salvation and whether or not the Lord would ever forsake her. Her father had left her and her mother for another woman. She was eight years old at the time. Her mother, an alcoholic, left her with others for many years. Her boyfriend had just broken up with her. All of her security blankets were gone! She now had great doubts about her relationship to God. I shared the words of Jesus in John 10:28–29 with her, and they brought encouragement to her heart:

> "And I give them eternal life, and they shall never perish; neither shall anyone snatch them out of My hand. My Father, who has given them to Me, is greater than all; and no one is able to snatch them out of My Father's hand."

God's power is behind our security. Hebrews 13:5 quotes our Lord's words: "I will never leave you nor forsake you."

We need God's power for everything, although sometimes it takes a tragedy or heartache to show that fact to us. One friend I know never saw his need for God's power until his wife died. Then he went to pieces, and soon learned his need for God's power. We need God's power just to make it through the day, especially in our relationships with people. We need His power to overcome sinful habits and to live an abundant, happy, and fruitful Christian life. We need his power to witness to others, and in using our gifts and talents in His service. Stop kidding yourself—you need God's power all the time! Without it, we soon reveal our weaknesses and faults.

Questions to Ponder

1. What do we mean by omnipotence?
2. What things will God not do?
3. What evidences do you see of God's power?
4. Why do we need God's power in our lives?
5. Give one example in your life that shows your need of God's power. What are you doing about that need?

8

What Does God Know?

Does God know everything? The Bible says that God knows *all things* (1 John 3:20). That can be very threatening as well as reassuring, depending on what is going on in your life at the time.

Sometimes I wonder if God knows what I am doing or what I am thinking about doing. One sleepy summer day, as I was lying in the grass looking up at a clear blue sky with a few scattered white clouds passing by, I began to think about what God knows. I picked up a dandelion and proceeded to remove the leaves one by one. As I considered getting something cold to drink, I thought to myself, "I wonder if God knows what I want to do." As I picked the leaves off that dandelion, I said, after the first leaf, "I'm going to get that drink." The next leaf caused me to say, "I'm not going to get that drink." I said to God, "I'll bet You wonder how this is going to turn out, don't You?" After using up all my leaves, I started laughing, for I know that God even knew I would pick off the leaves of that dandelion and wonder about whether or not I would get a drink. (In case you are wondering—I got the drink, and God knew I would!)

Watching a replay of a football game on television reminds me somewhat of God's omniscience. He knows all things, even what is going to happen next. That is what I knew while watching the replay, because I saw the original, live performance of that football play.

What Is Included in the "All Things"?

"All" includes the intangible things like wisdom: "God understands its way, And He knows its place" (Job 28:23). God knows the material universe in a way none of us does. "He counts the number of the stars; He calls them all by name," says Psalm 147:4. That alone is an incredible insight into the infinite knowledge of God. To Job, God says, "Do you know the ordinances of the heavens?" (Job 38:33). God obviously does, and He continues his questioning of Job:

> "Do you know the time when the wild mountain goats bear young? Or can you mark when the deer gives birth? Can you number the months that they fulfill? Or do you know the time when they bear young?"
>
> Job 39:1–2

Matthew 10:29–30 reminds us that God knows when a sparrow falls to the ground and the number of hairs on our heads. What details! God knows all things.

God knows our days even before we experience them (Psalm 139:16), and is intimately acquainted with us even before we are born (Jeremiah 1:5). Isaiah 46:10 says that He declares "the end from the beginning, And from ancient times things that are not yet done." His knowledge spans all of time—past, present, and future.

God's knowledge extends to the dead (Job 26:5–6) as well as to all the living inhabitants of earth:

> The LORD looks from heaven; He sees all the sons of men. From the place of His habitation He looks On all the inhabitants of the earth; He fashions their hearts individually; He considers all their works.
>
> Psalm 33:13–15

The Psalmist exalts the knowledge of God when he says:

O LORD, You have searched me and known me. You know my sitting down and my rising up; You understand my thought afar off. You comprehend my path and my lying down, And are acquainted with all my ways. For there is not a word on my tongue, But behold, O LORD, You know it altogether. You have hedged me behind and before, And laid Your hand upon me. Such knowledge is too wonderful for me; It is high, I cannot attain it.

Psalm 139:1–6

God's knowledge of us is all-inclusive—nothing is left out. As a young boy of ten, I was greatly tempted to steal a certain item out of a store in our neighborhood. It was something I really wanted. I argued to myself that they would not miss the item and could afford the loss. What bothered my conscience was the teaching of my parents that God knows all things. His knowledge of what I was thinking kept me that day from stealing. Though I have failed Him many times since, I am still aware today (even more so) that there is nothing I do, say, or think that escapes His knowledge.

When the apostles of our Lord met to replace Judas who hanged himself, they faced a difficult decision. There were two men among the disciples of Jesus who met the qualifications: Joseph, called Barsabas, with a surname of Justus, and a man named Matthias. They prayed to God: "You, O Lord, who know the hearts of all, show which of these two You have chosen" (Acts 1:24). They then cast lots (a method of voting) and Matthias was chosen.

Hebrews 4:13 tells us: "And there is no creature hidden from His sight, but all things are naked and open to the eyes of Him to whom we must give account." Proverbs 15:3 adds: "The eyes of the LORD are in every place, Keeping watch on the evil and the good." No one is really getting away with anything. God knows all we think, say, and do.

God also knows who are true believers and who are not: "For the LORD knows the way of the righteous" (Psalm 1:6). We also read: "The Lord knows those who are His" (2 Timothy 2:19). Jesus is quoted as saying, "My sheep hear My voice, and I know them, and they follow Me" (John 10:27). That is reassuring to the believer as it relates to our future and our security.

God knows all things from beginning to end. He is not surprised by any turn of events. The circumstances of our lives are all known to Him, not only in terms of the event which is happening, but also in terms of why it happens.

How Does It Affect Us?

When we say that God knows everything, it has some practical implications as to what we think, say, and do. Much of our immaturity is directly traceable to our misunderstanding or misapplication of God's omniscience. To know that He knows is the beginning of knowledge itself:

> Yes, if you cry out for discernment, And lift up your voice for understanding, If you seek for her as silver, And search for her as for hidden treasures; Then you will understand the fear of the LORD, *And find the knowledge of God.* For the LORD gives wisdom; From His mouth come knowledge and understanding.
>
> Proverbs 2:3–6

We read in Proverbs 9:10 that "the knowledge of the Holy One is understanding." To know Him is to understand; to ignore Him is to remain in darkness.

The Need for Honesty

Nothing so generates the honesty of the soul as the firm conviction that what you are hiding is known to others. In a home filled with teenagers, the phone got used! Every month when the phone bill came around, we had a few discussions about its use. It was always interesting to me how dishonest we were about phone calls we had made (long-distance charges), until the knowledge of the number called, the date it was called, and the confirmation of who made the call was revealed. Then there was an outpouring of honesty and confession. (The real problem for our teenagers, of course, was the knowledge that they would have to pay for those long-distance calls to their friends.)

Your character is what God knows you to be—your reputation is only what people think you are. God knows what we are really like, so why be dishonest before Him? Do we really believe He does not see what we do or know what we say? This is a sobering matter: "For He knows deceitful men; He sees wickedness also. Will He not then consider it?" (Job 11:11). Psalm 44:21 reveals: "For He knows the secrets of the heart." Nothing in the deep recesses of our hearts escapes His knowledge. King David learned that lesson the hard way. He committed adultery with Bathsheba and arranged the death of her husband, thinking that no one knew. Then the Prophet Nathan exposed him. David wrote: "Behold, You desire truth in the inward parts, And in the hidden part You will make me to know wisdom" (Psalm 51:6).

Stop deceiving yourself about sinful thoughts and secret deeds—God knows! Psalm 69:5 declares, "O God, You know my foolishness; And my sins are not hidden from You." Can anything be more clear? Psalm 90:8 adds: "You have set our iniquities before You, Our secret sins in the light of Your countenance." Proverbs 15:3 reminds us: "The eyes of the LORD are in every place, Keeping watch on the evil and the good."

In Joshua 7, there is an important story about honesty and confession. Joshua had just begun the campaign to defeat the Canaanite strongholds in the land of Israel and take possession as God had commanded. At the city of Ai (a small place with few inhabitants) the people of Israel were defeated and shocked: ". . . the hearts of the people melted and became like water" (Joshua 7:5). The problem? A man named Achan had sinned against the Lord by taking some of the pagan spoils which God said to destroy. He hid them in his tent, thinking that no one would know. But God knows! In an incredible display of God's knowledge, lots were cast to determine the tribe, the family, the particular household, and finally the guilty person. Achan was exposed, and Joshua said: "My son, I beg you, give glory to the LORD God of Israel, and make confession to Him, and tell me now what you have done; do not hide it from me'' (Joshua 7:19). It glorifies God when we confess our sins instead of trying to hide or cover them: ''He who covers his sins will not prosper, But whoever confesses and forsakes them will have mercy'' (Proverbs 28:13).

Our refusal to be honest before God often affects others (as in the case of Achan's sin and Israel's defeat), even though we think it will not because no one knows. But God does!

The Need for Acceptance

Most of us think that if people really know what we are like, they will no longer accept us and love us, so we keep ''putting on.'' Because we want their approval, we try to impress others with what we do, as well as what we would not do.

The need for acceptance is powerful in all of us. Ephesians 1:6 includes these encouraging words for believers: ''He has made us accepted in the Beloved [One].'' Through our faith in Jesus Christ, we are accepted by God. Yet He knows what we are like! The Psalmist describes God's understanding of us:

> The LORD is merciful and gracious, Slow to anger, and abounding in mercy. He will not always strive with us, Nor will He keep His anger forever. He has not dealt with us according to our sins, Nor punished us according to our iniquities. For as the heavens are high above the earth, So great is His mercy toward those who fear Him; As far as the east is from the west, So far has He removed our transgressions from us. As a father pities his children, So the Lord pities those who fear Him. *For He knows our frame; He remembers that we are dust.*
>
> Psalm 103:8–14

He knows, but He still loves and accepts us—thanks to His patience and mercy.

Jenny was a girl who never felt accepted by her parents, who were perfectionists. She could never measure up and got into the practice of lying in order to make people accept her and respond to her. She was greatly troubled that people would find out about her failures and faults and reject her. Jenny had some learning disabilities that made her feel quite insecure in most social settings. Fear, hurt, bitterness, suspicion, jealousy, insecurity—all these emotions and more were her daily diet. When I shared with her that God knows all about her, including all that she was hiding inside, she became very fearful at first. She thought God, therefore, must reject her if He really knows her. I assured Jenny that such was not the case, since God's knowledge brings God's loving understanding. She was especially excited about the passage quoted above from Psalm 103. Slowly but surely, she began to relax in the full acceptance of God and His love for her, and her relationships with people began to thrive and develop. God's knowledge can be frightening if we are trying to hide, but wonderful if we know His love and forgiveness.

The Need for Trust

Because God knows all things, He can be trusted, and we can depend on Him in time of trial and need. A greater knowledge of God results in a greater trust in God. The more I know about God, the more I want to trust Him. It is very often the limited understanding of God or the myths people believe about God that makes them turn away from Him or be fearful to trust Him. There are several important areas of our lives where the knowledge of God leads us to trust Him. The following represent only a few of the reasons we can depend on Him.

1. Prayer: It is the spiritual air we breathe and vital to our relationship with God. Some of us ignore prayer, to our detriment, and others simply do not believe in it. Many do not know how to pray. Even the disciples of Jesus asked: "Lord, teach us to pray" (Luke 11:1). We all need to learn how to pray.

A fundamental need in prayer is that of faith or trust in God. Jesus says in Matthew 21:22: "And all things, whatever you ask in prayer, believing, you will receive." But can God be trusted? Will

He give you whatever you ask? When will He do it? Does He really hear your prayers, when He has so many others to hear?

First of all, our heavenly Father knows how we pray and why we pray. We are not deceiving Him. Jesus revealed this:

> "And when you pray, you shall not be like the hypocrites. For they love to pray standing in the synagogues and on the corners of the streets, that they may be seen by men. Assuredly, I say to you, they have their reward. But you, when you pray, go into your room, and when you have shut your door, pray to your Father who is in the secret place; and your Father who sees in secret will reward you openly. But when you pray, do not use vain repetitions as the heathen do. For they think that they will be heard for their many words. Therefore do not be like them. For your Father knows the things you have need of before you ask Him."
>
> Matthew 6:5–8

We observe that private prayer is better than public prayer, where the constant temptation exists to be seen by others. We learn that "in secret" our motives and requests are clearly seen by God and—with no one but Him to talk to or be seen by—we have a greater chance of being rewarded. We also do not need to repeat the same words or chants over and over again, as many pagan religions encourage. Though we may ask God about something again on another day (and should), we do not need to repeat ourselves within the context of one prayer. The reason? God knows what we need before we ask Him. So why pray at all?

One reason is that God commanded us to do it. Second, there is more to prayer than informing God of things we are not sure He knows. The fact is, God already knows our needs, but that eliminates neither the joy of talking to Him about them nor the need of getting our emotions clarified by talking to God. My greater need may be patience, peace, or trust, not simply receiving the answer to my first request. God's knowledge encourages me to pray, because I know that He knows my real needs. *I* don't—I may think I do, but truthfully, I don't!

Continuing this thought about God's knowing what we need before we ask Him, Jesus said:

> "Therefore do not worry, saying, 'What shall we eat?' or 'What shall we drink?' or 'What shall we wear?' For after all these things the Gentiles seek. For your heavenly Father knows that you need all these things. But seek first the kingdom of God and His righteousness, and all these things shall be added to you. Therefore do not worry about tomorrow, for tomorrow will worry about its own things. Sufficient for the day is its own trouble."
>
> Matthew 6:31–34

In this particular passage, God's knowledge eliminates worry and anxiety about what to eat, drink, or wear, and even about what tomorrow will be like. God can be trusted—so relax! This special sermon by Jesus Christ (The Sermon on the Mount) emphasizes true righteousness as compared with outward, external religious activity. Material needs and concerns about tomorrow do not represent the real priorities. God already knows about those matters. We need to seek first His kingdom and righteousness. The point is that God's knowledge not only eliminates undue concern for temporal matters, but also helps me to concentrate on the real priorities, because I know He will take care of my minor needs due to His knowledge of them. The real problem in many prayers, therefore, is concentration on the physical rather than the spiritual, the lesser priority over the greater one—all of which ignores the vast knowledge of God. Instead of trusting, we begin to worry. Once again, the root of most of our problems is a misunderstanding or misapplication of who God is and what He can do.

The woman was full of worry, and it was affecting her family and relationships with other people. I first noticed it in her prayers. In the home Bible study which she attended, we would often pray aloud—it was a learning time for all of us. When she prayed, her material needs were prominent, and she continued to repeat herself, displaying a great deal of nervous energy and frustration. When I asked her about it, she expressed great disappointment with prayer itself, since she had rarely seen God answer any of her prayers. After calming her down, I read Matthew 6 to her. When I finished and looked up at her, she was crying. I asked, ''What's wrong?'' She said, ''Why pray, when you can worry?'' I started to correct her, and she stopped me and said, ''I know how it goes. My problem is not trusting the Lord—He obviously knows all about my needs.'' She was her own best counselor. God's peace began to control her in the days ahead, and she seemed like a different woman. Her confidence grew as she began to focus on the God who knows, rather than on the needs she had.

2. *Suffering:* The knowledge of God can really help if you are presently going through some difficult times. When you are hurting, you often wonder if God knows and, most of all, if He cares. Psalm 31:7 speaks of God's knowledge in times of stress: ''I will be glad and rejoice in Your mercy, For You have considered my trouble; You have known my soul in adversities.'' The Psalmist also states:

> When my spirit was overwhelmed within me, Then You knew my path. In the way in which I walk They have secretly set a snare for me. Look on my right hand and see, For there is no one who acknowledges me; Refuge has failed me; No one cares for my soul.
>
> Psalm 142:3–4

There are times when all of us feel like that: ''No one cares for my soul.'' But God *knew my path,* even when *my spirit was overwhelmed within me.* The knowledge of God about my suffering is of great comfort to me.

Several years ago I had throat surgery. It was not a pleasant experience, and the pain after surgery was so intense that I wanted to end my life. It continued for weeks. Sometimes I cried uncontrollably and sometimes I screamed. In the midst of all that suffering, God's knowledge was an anchor to my soul. Though the pain was there, I knew He cared and that it was for my good. Indeed it was—not only physically by restoring my throat and voice, but spiritually by giving me a deeper understanding of the presence and knowledge of God in the midst of pain and suffering.

This is pointed out in 2 Peter 2:9: "The Lord knows how to deliver the godly out of temptations and to reserve the unjust under punishment for the day of judgment." We also read about: ". . . casting all your care upon Him, for He cares for you" (1 Peter 5:7).

3. Direction: All of us need direction—but where do we get it? To know what to do, where to go, how to do it—these are the common perplexities of our lives. We face questions like these every day. Sometimes they loom large in our minds: Should you take that job across the country that promises higher pay but uproots your family? Should you marry this person, even when there are doubts in your mind and heart? Should you invest in this project, even though there is great risk in the midst of great potential?

Life is filled with the need for direction. One of the greatest effects on my life in this area has been the infinite knowledge of God. He knows the way! Consider the evidence:

Job 23:10—"But *He knows the way* that I take; When He has tested me, I shall come forth as gold."

Psalm 1:6—"For *the Lord knows the way* of the righteous."

Psalm 32:8—"I will instruct you and teach you in *the way* you should go; I will guide you with My eye."

Psalm 37:5—"Commit *your way* to the LORD, Trust also in Him, And He shall bring it to pass."

Psalm 37:18—"*The Lord knows* the days of the upright, And their inheritance shall be forever."

The way I should go is often not observable to me, because I do not trust in God's sovereign care and knowledge. If He knows the way, then His way is what I need to follow: "Wait on the LORD, And keep *His way*" (Psalm 37:34). The way of the Lord is often revealed through His Word—that gives clear direction. His vast knowledge of all things allows Him to communicate (in the Bible) eternal principles that govern all decision making throughout all time. Only an omniscient God could arrange that!

Psalm 119:1 says, "Blessed are the undefiled in *the way,* Who walk in the law of the LORD!" In verse 5, the Psalmist cries, "Oh, that *my ways* were directed To keep Your statutes!" Obviously, God's Word directs our ways: "I will meditate on Your precepts, And contemplate *Your ways*" (verse 15), and verse 27 brings forth this prayer of the heart: "Make me understand *the way* of Your precepts." Verse 33 adds, "Teach me, O LORD, *the way* of Your statutes. . . ." Psalm 119 is filled with such emphasis. The way we should go is the way of the Lord, as revealed in His Word, the Bible. I need to trust the God who knows the way I should go and what I should do.

4. Understanding: Sometimes I need to understand. Take computers, for instance. I don't understand them, but I want to, and in some respects I need to. I am just starting to learn about them, and the fear is going away. Now I am getting excited about their potential. We usually fear what we do not understand. Fear is the opposite of trust. It is difficult for me to trust something or someone that I do not really understand. God's knowledge is helpful here. He understands everything, and the more I understand and know Him, the more I understand about life and myself: ". . . the knowledge of the Holy One is understanding" (Proverbs 9:10).

Hebrews 11:3 tells us that "by faith we understand that the worlds were framed by the word of God." Belief is essential to understanding. I must believe in God and His Word, the Bible, in order to gain understanding of such difficult issues as the origin of the solar system.

Understanding of God's ways with His people Israel has not always been clear. The Apostle Paul discussed these problems in some detail in Romans 9–11 and concluded the whole discussion with these marvelous words about God's knowledge:

> Oh, the depth of the riches both of the wisdom and knowledge of God! How unsearchable are His judgments and His ways past finding out! "For who has known the mind of the LORD? Or who has become His counselor? Or who has first given to Him And it shall be repaid to him?" For of Him and

through Him and to Him are all things, to whom be glory
forever. Amen.

Romans 11:33–36

My understanding demands trust in the God who knows all things.
The more I know of Him and His ways, the clearer things become
and the more I understand.

Prayer, suffering, direction, and understanding—each requires
trust in the infinite wisdom and knowledge of God. To believe that
God does not know certain things is not only to insult Him, but to
leave us helpless and hopeless in these matters of practical concern.

When we observe the greatness of God's knowledge, it brings
out our needs—needs for honesty, acceptance, and trust. But there
is one more thing . . .

The Need for Thankfulness and Praise

Paul wrote in Romans 11:36, after mentioning the infinite
knowledge of God: *To whom be glory forever. Amen.* Do you
glorify God, the God who knows all things? The Psalmist David
shared his heart when he wrote: "How precious also are Your
thoughts to me, O God! How great is the sum of them!" (Psalm
139:17). In the same chapter, he said, "Such knowledge is too
wonderful for me; It is high, I cannot attain it" (verse 6). *Precious—wonderful*—these are words of praise to God for the knowledge He has.

Daniel praised the Lord for His knowledge and what pos-
sibilities were therefore available to him in revealing the dream of
Nebuchadnezzar, King of Babylon—"So Daniel blessed the God
of heaven" (Daniel 2:19). Here's what he said:

> "Blessed be the name of God forever and ever, For wisdom
> and might are His. And He changes the times and the sea-
> sons; He removes kings and raises up kings; He gives
> wisdom to the wise And knowledge to those who have under-
> standing. He reveals deep and secret things; He knows what

is in the darkness, And light dwells with Him. I thank You
and praise You, O God of my fathers; You have given me
wisdom and might, And have now made known to me what
we asked of You, For You have made known to us the king's
demand."

Daniel 2:20–23

Colossians 2:3 says of Jesus Christ, ". . . in whom are hidden all
the treasures of wisdom and knowledge." Paul writes in Ephesians
3:17–21 about the love of Christ that—if we know it—we will
discover that it surpasses certain levels of knowledge. He ends the
discussion by saying, ". . . to Him be glory in the church by
Christ Jesus throughout all ages, world without end. Amen"
(verse 21).

Knowing that God knows all things should bring out our praise
and thanksgiving. Praise the Lord that He knows—somebody
surely needs to know! I am so grateful that a just and loving God
knows it all. Because of who He is, His vast knowledge is worth
trusting at all times—Hallelujah!

Questions to Ponder

1. What is included in the "all things" that God knows?
2. How does God's omniscience affect our attitude toward sin?
3. Why is honesty such a great need with all of us?
4. How does God's knowledge bring a sense of acceptance and
worth to us?
5. In what areas do we need to trust God's knowledge?
6. Why pray—if God already knows?
7. How does God's knowledge help us in the matter of direction for our lives?

9

Can We Trust God?

A girl in her twenties was sitting at the counter of a restaurant in Iowa where I stopped for a meal. She looked terrible and had obviously not had a bath or shampoo in weeks. She smelled, and her eyes were bloodshot. She asked me for a smoke, which, of course, I did not have. Instead, I asked her where she was from. She said, "Nowhere." Then I asked, "Where are you going?" Again she said, "Nowhere." I finally asked, "What's wrong?" She turned and looked intently at me and began to cry uncontrollably. Her parents had divorced when she was a young child and she was put into a special institution for girls whom no one really wanted. Although her parents were church members and had even taken her to Sunday school, they rarely came to see her while she was in that institution. When old enough to be on her own, she hit the streets, wandering from town to town. She had been misused and abused through various sexual encounters and promises—an old story, but it still hurts to hear it again. She had lost all confidence in anyone or anything and did not trust me either. As I began to tell her about God's love for her, she asked, "Can He be trusted?" I answered, "Of course. He's God!" She countered, "Why should I trust Him? Everyone else has let me down!"

To make a long story short, this young woman became a Christian, and a fine Christian couple took her in and loved her as she had never known before. She learned to trust God and His people who cared for her.

Life is filled with many heartaches and disappointments. God seems so far away, and you often are not sure what He can or will do about your situation. Can He really be trusted? Upon what evidence do we say that He can?

When a friend lost his job, I watched his trust in God slowly deteriorate. He was losing faith in a God who cares—because He saw little evidence of God's concern. He was out looking for work every day for a while, but soon gave up. He became depressed and started drinking. The bottle became his relief medicine, as his trust in God was replaced by the sedative of alcohol. What a tragedy! Does God care when you lose your job? Can He be trusted to do something about it?

The Basis of Trust

What causes us to trust anyone? When we are small children, it seems we have a natural instinct to trust our parents until their actions or words prove otherwise. Do we trust people simply because they are figures of authority? Do we trust the doctor to whom we must go for physical help? Do we trust our political and civic leaders? Do we trust our pastors? What is the basis of trust? How does it apply to God?

I see three factors that are necessary in order to build trust in someone.

- A person must tell the truth.
- A person must do right and be fair or just.
- A person must be dependable or reliable.

In my opinion, these three factors are necessary if real trust in that person is to exist. It is interesting that these important qualities are found in three attributes of God to which the Bible often points us.

1. God is holy—He will not lie to us.
2. God is just—He will always do right.

3. God is faithful—He is always dependable.

God Is Holy!

In some respects, this is the major attribute of God. According to Isaiah 6:3, the angels of God cry: "Holy, holy, holy is the LORD of hosts; The whole earth is full of His glory!"

The Hebrew word (*kadesh*) and the Greek word (*hagios*) for the English word *holy* mean "that which is separate." God is separate in two ways. He is separate from all that He created—and He is separate from all that is unclean or sinful. One deals with His greatness or majesty, and the other, His moral purity.

God is separate from His creation: "The LORD is great in Zion, And He is high above all the peoples. Let them praise Your great and awesome name—He is holy" (Psalm 99:2–3).

God is *high above all the peoples.* His holiness separates Him from His creatures. According to verse 5, our response should be . . . "Exalt the LORD our God, And worship at His footstool; For He is holy." Verse 9 repeats the same thought: "Exalt the LORD our God, And worship at His holy hill; For the Lord our God is holy." In verse 5, we worship at His *footstool* and in verse 9, at His *holy hill.*

Isaiah 57:15 says that God is "the High and Lofty One Who inhabits eternity, whose name is Holy." Again the emphasis is on His exalted position—His separateness from all His creation.

Psalm 105:42 speaks of "His holy promise" to Abraham, and Psalm 98:1 tells us of "His holy arm" that has gained Him the victory. Psalm 47:8 tells of "His holy throne" from which He reigns over the nations, and Psalm 48:1 speaks of "His holy mountain," Mount Zion, the city of the great King.

Deuteronomy 26:15 says, "Look down from Your holy habitation, from heaven, and bless Your people Israel." Once again God's separateness from His people is emphasized. He is not like us in terms of holiness, though we are like Him in personality. He is separate and shall ever remain so. The Creator is not to be confused with, nor lowered to, His creation.

Israel is separate from other nations: Leviticus tells us that offerings which Israel gave to God were holy or separate:

> Nevertheless no devoted offering that a man may devote to the LORD of all that he has, both man and beast, or the field of his possession, shall be sold or redeemed; every devoted offering is most holy to the LORD.
>
> Leviticus 27:28

Also according to Leviticus, certain foods were off limits to the people of Israel. God gave them a special diet to make them "holy" or separate from all the nations around them. It would remind them that they were the Lord's people:

> "For I am the LORD your God. You shall therefore sanctify yourselves, and you shall be holy; for I am holy. Neither shall you defile yourselves with any creeping thing that creeps on the earth. For I am the LORD Who brings you up out of the land of Egypt, to be your God. You shall therefore be holy, for I am holy."
>
> Leviticus 11:44–45

Deuteronomy makes these interesting demands of God's people:

> "You are the children of the LORD your God; you shall not cut yourselves nor shave the front of your head for the dead. For you are a holy people to the LORD your God, and the LORD has chosen you to be a people for Himself, a special treasure above all the peoples who are on the face of the earth."
>
> Deuteronomy 14:1–2

After further instruction about what to eat and not eat, God adds: "For you are a holy people to the LORD your God" (verse 21). Israel was to be separate from other nations by diet as well as many other practices and observances. Their holiness did not refer to their moral purity, but to their peculiar practices. They were to be different and separate from the nations around them.

God's creatures are not always reliable, as many of us have frequently found out! People will disappoint you and let you down. That is why God's holiness is so important. He is separate from His creation and unlike them in so many ways.

The importance of moral purity: The major idea people usually have when thinking about holiness is moral purity—being separate from all that is sinful or unclean. That is absolutely essential if God is to be trusted:

> "Who may ascend into the hill of the LORD? Or who may stand in His holy place? He who has clean hands and a pure heart, Who has not lifted up his soul to an idol, Nor sworn deceitfully."
>
> Psalm 24:3–4

Holiness demands "clean hands and a pure heart." There can be no deceit or idolatry.

God's holiness means that there is no sin in Him at all. He is incapable of committing a sin and will never do any wrong. Hebrews 6:18 says that "it is impossible for God to lie." That is the foundation of His trustworthiness—He will not lie! In 1 John 1:5, we read: "God is light and in Him is no darkness at all."

Because God is holy, He demands holiness in His people, as 1 Peter 1:15–16 says: "But as He who called you is holy, you also be holy in all your conduct, because it is written, 'Be holy, for I am holy.'" God said that frequently to His people Israel (Leviticus 11:44–45; 19:2; 20:7). Hebrews 12:14 tells us to pursue holiness, "without which no one will see the Lord."

One of the important biblical texts dealing with the need of holiness or separation among God's people is found in 2 Corinthians:

> Do not be unequally yoked together with unbelievers. For what fellowship has righteousness with lawlessness? And

what communion has light with darkness? And what accord has Christ with Belial? Or what part has a believer with an unbeliever? And what agreement has the temple of God with idols? For you are the temple of the living God. As God has said: "I will dwell in them And walk among them. I will be their God, And they shall be My people." Therefore "Come out from among them And be separate, says the Lord. Do not touch what is unclean, And I will receive you. I will be a Father to you, And you shall be My sons and daughters, says the Lord Almighty." Therefore, having these promises, beloved, let us cleanse ourselves from all filthiness of the flesh and spirit, perfecting holiness in the fear of God."`

2 Corinthians 6:14–7:1

Here is taught separation from unbelievers, as well as separation from "all filthiness of the flesh and spirit." When we say that God is holy, we mean that He is totally separate from sin in every way. Because of that, we can trust Him.

Psalm 89 indicates that God's holiness backs up the veracity of His promises:

"My covenant I will not break, Nor alter the word that has gone out of My lips. Once I have sworn by My holiness; I will not lie to David; His seed shall endure forever, and his throne as the sun before Me; It shall be established forever like the moon, Even like the faithful witness in the sky."

Psalm 89:34–37

God swears by the fact of His separateness from all creation and sin. That means He will do what He has said. He is absolutely trustworthy because of it!

After I spoke at a Bible conference in the Midwest on the subject of sin and what to do about it, a woman approached me with tears in her eyes and asked, "Will God really forgive us for what we have done?" She went on to say that as a result of an affair she had with another man besides her husband, she has been filled with guilt and doubts about her salvation. She had confessed her sin and truly repented, but she did not feel forgiven. She wanted assurance that God had forgiven her. She asked, "Can adultery be forgiven?" I asked, "What does the Bible say?" She said, "Well, I know it says that, but how do we know for sure?" I then told her that her problem was in not trusting God to do what He says. I reminded her that He does not lie. If He said He would forgive, then that settles it! We had prayer together, and she confessed to God how sorry she was for not believing His Word. God's peace filled her heart immediately. Her problem was centered in her lack of confidence in God. God's holy character guarantees that He is trustworthy—He will not lie to us. Praise the Lord!

God Is Just!

In order to trust someone, you must believe that he or she will do right. Justice and fairness are essential. One high school student I talked with had great difficulty in trusting one of his coaches. The boy's attitude was bad, and he knew it. His coach had made a decision to put him on the bench, believing that this boy was guilty of something he never did. As a result, the boy lost confidence in his coach. He could not be trusted. I tried to explain to him that his coach was only human and thus could make mistakes. That did not seem to help this young athlete. All he saw was the injustice. It was just "not fair." Life is like that. This reminded me of the importance of justice in the nature of God. Genesis 18:25 asks, "Shall not the Judge of all the earth do right?"

The Hebrew word (*tsadik*) means "straight." There are no crooked dealings by God—no deviation from what is right to do. He always does right. Therefore, He can be trusted.

The Book of Psalms continually affirms God's righteousness: "For the LORD is righteous, He loves righteousness" (Psalm 11:7). We read also that the "statutes of the LORD are right, rejoicing the heart" (Psalm 19:8)—"You love righteousness and hate wickedness" (Psalm 45:7). "Righteousness and justice are the foundation of Your throne" (Psalm 89:14), and "Righteous are You, O LORD, And upright are Your judgments" (Psalm 119:137). Perhaps one of the greatest statements about the justice of God is in Psalm 145:17: "The LORD is righteous in all His ways, Gracious in all His works." What encouragement to our hearts! Jeremiah 50:7 calls the Lord "the habitation of justice."

He will keep His promises! Ezra appealed to God's righteous character when confessing the sins of the people of Israel, as well as rejoicing that God had left a remnant to return to the land:

> "O LORD God of Israel, You are righteous, for we are left a remnant, as it is this day. Here we are before You, in our guilt, though no one can stand before You because of this!"
>
> Ezra 9:15

Because God is righteous, His promise to Israel was kept in spite of their sin and disobedience. A remnant was spared. God will do right. If He promised something and it was based not on human performance but on His own veracity, then He will and must keep His word:

> "Gather My saints together to Me, Those who have made a covenant with Me by sacrifice." Let the heavens declare His righteousness, For God Himself is Judge.
>
> Psalm 50:5–6

God's righteousness guarantees that He will keep His covenant.

He will judge those who do wrong: In his prayer to God, Daniel confesses the sin of his people and the righteousness of God in judging them:

> "Therefore the LORD has kept the disaster in mind, and brought it upon us; for the LORD our God is righteous in all the works which He does, though we have not obeyed His voice."
>
> Daniel 9:14

People often ask about the justice of God when they see the wickedness of this world. Good people often suffer, and wicked people seem to be getting away with their terrible deeds. Where is God in all of this? Can He be trusted to rectify these things?

Beloved, do not avenge yourselves, but rather give place to wrath; for it is written, "Vengeance is Mine, I will repay," says the Lord.

Romans 12:19

The Book of Revelation pictures a scene in heaven in the future when the seven last plagues are being introduced. Believers in heaven are singing the song of Moses and the song of the Lamb:

"Great and marvelous are Your works, Lord God Almighty! Just and true are Your ways, O King of the saints! Who shall not fear You, O Lord, and glorify Your name? For You alone are holy. For all nations shall come and worship before You, For Your judgments have been manifested."

Revelation 15:3–4

When one of the angels pours out the wrath of God in one of the seven last plagues, we read this:

"You are righteous, O Lord, The One who is and who was and who is to be, Because You have judged these things. For they have shed the blood of saints and prophets, And You have given them blood to drink. For it is their just due."

Revelation 16:5–6

Another voice from the altar says in verse 7: "Even so, Lord God Almighty, true and righteous are Your judgments."

Because you can trust God to judge those who do wrong, no one will get away with anything.

He will forgive us: God's justice demands that we be forgiven of our sins if certain conditions are met. According to 1 Peter 3:18: "For Christ also suffered once for sins, the just for the unjust, that He might bring us to God, being put to death in the flesh but made alive by the Spirit." Romans 3:26 says that God's righteousness was demonstrated when Jesus died for our sins, "that He might be just and the justifier of the one who has faith in Jesus."

We read in 1 John 1:9: "If we confess our sins, He is faithful and just to forgive us our sins and to cleanse us from all unrighteousness.'' God's justice makes our forgiveness possible because Jesus died in our place—praise the Lord! Therefore, God can be completely trusted. He is just.

He will never forget our work: God is so trustworthy that you can count on Him to reward whatever you have done for Him. His justice is behind it:

> For God is not unjust to forget your work and labor of love which you have shown toward His name, in that you have ministered to the saints, and do minister.
>
> Hebrews 6:10

Many people do not believe that anyone notices, much less cares about what they do. God, who is just, is One who cares. Nothing escapes His notice. He remembers—He will not forget. I shared that with a dear woman whose job was not usually noticed. She often washed dishes in the church kitchen for banquets and began to feel that no one cared. While walking through the kitchen one night while she was working, I shared Hebrews 6:10 with her, and her eyes brightened. She asked, ''Do you mean that God notices my washing these dishes?'' I said, ''No doubt about it' What's more, He will reward you for your faithfulness to Him, even though no one else ever notices what you have done.'' God cares—because He is just!

God Is Faithful!

Proverbs 17:17 says, ''A friend loves at all times, And a brother is born for adversity.'' It is hard to find faithful friends these days. Everyone seems to be doing his or her own thing. Where are your friends when you need them?

I asked an elderly woman, crippled by arthritis, what she wanted most. The loneliness of that convalescent hospital was difficult for her. She answered, ''A faithful friend.'' She continued, ''Without the Lord, I don't know what I'd do. My friends don't come by much anymore.''

The whole matter of trust is sometimes based solely on the faithfulness of the person you want to trust. Without dependability, it is difficult to trust. God is dependable. The depth of that fact is rooted in the immutability of His character. The Bible teaches that He does not change; therefore, you can depend on Him.

God does not change: All the changes in man and his circumstances do not alter or affect the unchangeableness of God. His character and plans remain the same from the beginning of time and creation. And His actions are always consistent with His own nature and purposes:

> Every good gift and every perfect gift is from above, and comes down from the Father of lights, with whom there is no variation or shadow of turning.
>
> James 1:17

This clearly tells us that the planetary bodies are directly controlled by our heavenly Father. They move and cast shadows, depending on their relationship to the sun or stars. According to this verse, it is not so with God. He is unchangeable, and as 1 John 1:5 says: "In Him is no darkness at all." According to the Psalmist:

> God is our refuge and strength, A very present help in trouble. Therefore we will not fear, Though the earth be removed, And though the mountains be carried into the midst of the sea; Though its waters roar and be troubled, Though the mountains shake with its swelling.
>
> Psalm 46:1–3

The clear point of that passage is that God will not change in terms of being our help in time of trouble. Even though the earth, its mountains, and its seas would be changed, God would still be there to help us. What a blessed promise that passage is to our hearts!

> Of old You laid the foundation of the earth, And the heavens are the work of Your hands. They will perish, but You will endure; Yes, all of them will grow old like a garment; Like a

cloak You will change them, And they will be changed. But
You are the same, And Your years will have no end.

Psalm 102:25–27

This passage clearly tells us that although the material creation will
perish, God Himself will continue to endure. They will be
changed, but God will remain the same. His unchangeableness is a
guarantee to us of His dependability and reliability.

What God does change is based on His unchanging character
and plan. According to Acts 17:26, the very times of nations are
predetermined and even the boundaries of their habitations. But
Daniel 2:21 says that God changes the times and the seasons.
When we say that God does not change, that does not mean that
He does not change things. Man's performance does not change
God's character or plan. God's response to man's performance is
always consistent with what He said and who He is. Changing
circumstances in our lives are not the result of chance or coincidence. Proverbs 16:33 says: "The lot is cast into the lap, But its
every decision is from the LORD." To this is added: "And we
know that all things work together for good to those who love
God, to those who are the called according to His purpose" (Romans 8:28).

Knowing the immutability of God's character should continue
to build our trust and confidence in the Lord. It is the foundation
behind God's faithfulness. It will be relatively easy to trust God
in difficult situations if we are convinced that He is the faithful
God who will never leave us nor forsake us.

What the Bible says about the faithfulness of God. One of the
most important passages dealing with our understanding of God's
faithfulness to us is found in Deuteronomy, chapter 7. Here the
Bible tells us why God chose Israel above all the other nations of
the earth. He explains that He did this, not because they were
great in numbers, but because He wanted to demonstrate something about His love and His faithfulness to us:

"Therefore know that the LORD your God, He is God, the

faithful God who keeps covenant and mercy for a thousand generations with those who love Him and keep His commandments."

Deuteronomy 7:9

When we go to the Psalms, we are reminded frequently of the faithfulness of God: "Your mercy, O LORD, is in the heavens, And Your faithfulness reaches to the clouds" (Psalm 36:5). "Also with the lute I will praise you—And Your faithfulness, O my God!" (Psalm 71:22). The Psalmist specifically mentions the faithfulness of God as the subject of his musical praise:

> I will sing of the mercies of the LORD forever; With my mouth will I make known Your faithfulness to all generations. For I have said, "Mercy shall be built up forever; Your faithfulness You shall establish in the very heavens."
>
> Psalm 89:1-2

Later in that same chapter, we read: "Nevertheless My loving-kindness I will not utterly take from him, nor allow My faithfulness to fail" (verse 33). It is obvious that God is so faithful, that He will never fail to keep His word and His promise to us. Lamentations 3:22–23 are precious verses to every believer: "Through the LORD's mercies we are not consumed, Because His compassions fail not. They are new every morning; Great is Your faithfulness." It is obvious from that passage that our very lives are dependent upon the faithfulness of God in extending His loving mercy toward us. His compassion never fails and, therefore, His faithfulness is described as being "great."

What God's Faithfulness Means to Us Today

It is very crucial to our ability to trust God to understand what His faithfulness means to us today. The impact of these great promises in the Bible will affect the way we see things and the way we respond to difficult circumstances. God can be trusted because He is the faithful God.

1. It Helps Us in Time of Temptation

A passage in 1 Corinthians is of great blessing to the believer. There are times when we are tempted to such an extent that we wonder if we have the ability to endure, but: "No temptation has overtaken you except such as is common to man; but God is faithful, who will not allow you to be tempted beyond what you are able, but with the temptation will also make the way of escape, that you may be able to bear it" (1 Corinthians 10:13). God never puts on us more than we can bear. The reason? He is the faithful God.

In talking with a young college student one day, I discovered that he was involved in sexual sin. He said to me that the temptations he experienced were greater than what he was able to endure. In reality, he was blaming God for putting him in the position where he found himself falling into sin. But the Bible is careful in telling us that God does not tempt any man to sin (James 1:13). And 1 Corinthians 10:13 clearly teaches that because God is faithful to us, He will never allow the temptations to be greater than what we can bear.

2. It Protects Us from the Evil One

We read in 2 Thessalonians 3:3: "But the Lord is faithful, who will establish you and guard you from the evil one." The previous two verses deal with the importance of trusting God as we share the Word of God with people. There are unreasonable and wicked people whom we must face from time to time. We are to have courage and to know that God is faithful and will guard us from the attempts of Satan to defeat our testimony and witness.

3. It Guarantees Forgiveness and Cleansing

"If we confess our sins, He is faithful and just to forgive us our sins and to cleanse us from all unrighteousness" (1 John 1:9). What a blessed assurance that verse is to our hearts! God is faithful and therefore must forgive us on the basis of our faith in His Son, Jesus Christ. The death and resurrection of Jesus Christ are still efficacious today to all who believe. God remains faithful to what Christ has done for us already. Therefore, we can be forgiven and cleansed from our sins if we will confess our sins— which means to agree with God as to what He says about them.

4. It Gives Us Security for the Future

We have this assurance: "Now may the God of peace Himself sanctify you completely; and may your whole spirit, soul, and body be preserved blameless at the coming of our Lord Jesus Christ. He who calls you is faithful, who also will do it" (1 Thessalonians 5:23–24). Because God is a faithful God, we can count on Him to accomplish His work in us and protect us until the coming of our Lord and Saviour, Jesus Christ. Hebrews 10:23 adds to this by saying, "Let us hold fast the confession of our hope without wavering, for He who promised is faithful." This gives us encouragement to "stay with the stuff," as it were, knowing that God is faithful and will keep His promises to us. Our future is secure because God is a faithful God. We also have this remarkable assurance in 2 Timothy 2:13: "If we are faithless, He remains faithful; He cannot deny Himself." The faithful God guarantees our security. The assurance that we will one day be with the Lord forever is based on who God is and not on our performance.

Questions to Ponder

1. What three factors are necessary in order to build trust in someone?
2. What do we mean when we say that God is holy?
3. How does the holiness of God help us to trust Him?
4. What does it mean to us when we say that God is just?
5. What do we mean by the immutability of God's character?
6. What does God's faithfulness do for us today?

10

Does God Really Care?

Rabbi Harold Kushner, in his best-selling book, *When Bad Things Happen to Good People,* has forcibly brought the issue about God's love and care to all our minds and hearts. The author is concerned about suffering and tragedy and about who God is and what He can do. On page 134, he writes these words:

> I believe in God. But I do not believe the same things about Him that I did years ago, when I was growing up or when I was a theological student. I recognize His limitations. He is limited in what He can do by laws of nature and by the evolution of human nature and human moral freedom. I no longer hold God responsible for illnesses, accidents, and natural disasters, because I realize that I gain little and I lose so much when I blame God for those things. I can worship a God who hates suffering but cannot eliminate it, more easily than I can worship a God who chooses to make children suffer and die, for whatever exalted reason. Some years ago, when the "death of God" theology was a fad, I remember seeing a bumper sticker that read, "My God is not dead; sorry about yours." I guess my bumper sticker reads, "My God is not cruel; sorry about yours."*

Rabbi Kushner is writing out of personal experience. He lost a

---

* *When Bad Things Happen to Good People* (New York: Avon Books, 1981), p. 134.

son through the illness of progeria. During that time, his soul was deeply stirred as he evaluated God's role in the matter. His sensitivity and understanding are appreciated by all who read his book. But in my mind still lingers the question about his understanding of God. His personal experience has affected his understanding. We must never allow our experiences to govern what the Bible actually teaches concerning the character and actions of God. The God of Rabbi Kushner is limited; the God of the Bible is not. Rabbi Kushner is deeply disturbed about God's failure to solve the problems of human suffering, but the Bible teaches that God has His reasons and that suffering can be a blessing. Much can be gained and learned through those experiences, and the Bible teaches that ultimately—when Jesus Christ comes back again—all pain, suffering, sorrow, sickness, and death will be gone forever. Our hope does not lie in this life, but in the life to come.

But does God really care? I mean, does He really care about what I am going through? Am I just a part of His great cosmic plan and the "all things" that God is bringing to a great climax without any assurance of love, understanding, and concern from Him? I believe that the Bible teaches that God is personally concerned about all that transpires in our lives. He really cares. He is a loving and merciful God and understands our weaknesses, limitations and temptations. Furthermore, His strength and power are available to all who call upon Him. He can sustain us in the darkness and the pain, bringing comfort to our hearts when our sorrow seems almost unbearable. God's love is continually presented in the Scriptures as not only a fact, but a great blessing to all who will trust Him.

While eating in a restaurant, the waitress for our table told us she was having a "rough day." Everything seemed to be going wrong. I asked her if there was anything happening in her life that might be causing her to evaluate that day as being difficult. She then began to tell me about the problems she was having. Her husband was divorcing her; he was in love with another woman. Her mother and father were blaming her. Her husband had already moved out of the house and was not providing any financial help for her and the children. She was very discouraged, lonely, bitter, and hostile, and when I began to tell her about the love of God, she looked at me with a cold stare and said, "I don't believe that God really cares about me." It was obvious, as we continued to talk, that she had reasons for her viewpoint. But what I noticed that day about this waitress, I have seen so many times before. That is, that most people do not know the God of the Bible. They relate to Him only by what people have told them—people who say they believe in Him but do not show any love or care to others. That causes them to question whether God really loves and cares. Perhaps that is a valid comparison, but too much of the time, the people who say they believe in the God of the Bible do not know Him well themselves and, as a result, are poor testimonies for Him. The real questions are: "What does the Bible say about God? Does He really care?"

The Love of God

No other quality of God's character is so precious to the human soul than that of love. God's love will bring comfort and encouragement to the most depressed heart and discouraged life. God loves us in ways that most of us do not understand or ever appreciate. One of the great texts on the love of God is:

> Beloved, let us love one another, for love is of God; and everyone who loves is born of God and knows God. He who does not love does not know God, for God is love. In this the love of God was manifested toward us, that God has sent His only begotten Son into the world, that we might live through Him. In this is love, not that we loved God, but that He loved us and sent His Son to be the propitiation for our sins.
>
> 1 John 4:7–10

God is not merely love. When we speak of God's love as an essential part of His nature, it is only one side of the many attributes of God. His love would not be God's love if He were not a God of holiness and righteousness. His love never overlooks sin, but is consistent with all that God is and does. His love does not compromise with sin, nor tolerate it. It is not simply sympathy or sentimentality. According to this passage, God *is* love. That means that everything He does and says is bathed with the quality of love. He does not simply react to us apart from His essential loving nature. To say that God does not care about us is to deny who God really is. According to this portion of Scripture, our ability to love one another is based upon our personal knowledge of God Himself. It tells us that the greatest demonstration of God's love was sending His Son, Jesus Christ, into the world to die for our sins. According to John 3:16: "God so loved the world that He gave His only begotten Son." Romans 5:8 tells us: "But God demonstrates His own love toward us, in that while we were still sinners, Christ died for us."

God's love cares about us when we do not care anything about Him. God's love is unselfish; He always seeks the benefit of the object of His love. His love is voluntary; He gives to us before we ever give to Him: "We love Him because He first loved us" (1 John 4:19). God's love is also an everlasting love: "Yes, I have loved you with an everlasting love; Therefore with lovingkindness I have drawn you" (Jeremiah 31:3). We are reminded in 1 Corinthians 13:8 of the never-ending nature of God's love—"Love never fails." Love is the very essence of God's being.

Whom Does God Love?

The Bible is very clear as to the people toward whom God extends His love and those for whom He has great care and concern. It tells us that God loves His only begotten Son, Jesus Christ, in a special way. In Matthew 3:17 Jesus is called, by the Father, "My beloved Son." In John 3:35 it says very clearly that "the Father loves the Son." In John 17:24, in the great prayer of Jesus to His heavenly Father, He says, "For You loved Me before the foundation of the world."

The Bible also teaches that God loves those who love His Son and believe on Him. In John 16:27, we read: "For the Father

Himself loves you, because you have loved Me, and have believed that I came forth from God.'' These words are added in 1 John 3:1: ''Behold what manner of love the Father has bestowed on us, that we should be called children of God! Therefore the world does not know us, because it did not know Him.'' Yes, the Bible is very clear that God loves believers in a special way and especially because they love His Son, Jesus Christ.

The Bible also teaches that God has a special love for the nation of Israel. Deuteronomy 7:6–9 tells us of God's great love for Israel. He calls them a ''special treasure above all the peoples on the face of the earth.'' We learn in this passage that God chose them because He loved them. Jeremiah 31:3–4 is applied to the nation of Israel when God says that He loves them and ''with lovingkindness'' has ''drawn'' them to Himself. Verse 4 specifically says that this love refers to the ''virgin of Israel.''

The Bible also teaches that God loves the entire world and every person in it. One of the favorite verses of many Christians is John 3:16: ''For God so loved the world that He gave His only begotten Son, that whoever believes in Him should not perish but have everlasting life.'' God loves sinners and people who reject Him as surely as He loves the believers who come to receive Jesus Christ as their Lord and Saviour. Obviously, He loves believers in a special way in comparison with His love for those who reject Him. It is also obvious that He loves His Son, Jesus Christ, in a special sense that separates Him from all those who believe in Him. God's love reaches out to all. The very word *love,* we are told in 1 John 4:7, comes out of the very nature of God Himself. Any real love in the world must center itself back, in terms of origin and roots, into the nature and character of God Himself.

How Does God Show His Love?

Many people need to see a demonstration of the love of God. You can tell them all day that God loves them, but until they see the evidence of it, they simply do not believe it. My wife feels that way concerning the times when I tell her, ''I love you.'' When I do things that demonstrate that love, it makes her feel loved, even though she still likes to hear the words. It is important that we say the words, but it is much more important that we back up our words with actions.

One day my wife was not feeling well and was confined to bed because of the flu. I came home from the office early that day and cleaned the house, prepared dinner for the kids, and did everything I possibly could to take care of the daily routine that she does when she is well. The next day, after she was feeling much better, she wrote me the sweetest note and sent it to me by way of sticking it in my briefcase. When I got to the office and opened the briefcase, the note shared how much she felt my love for her because of all I had done for her while she was sick. Once again, we will convince people that we truly love them when we show that love by our actions. God also shows and demonstrates His love toward us in many ways.

1. He shows that His love is impartial whenever it rains.

Matthew 5:43–48 describes the importance of loving our enemies: ". . . for He makes His sun rise on the evil and on the good, and sends rain on the just and on the unjust" (verse 45). The fact that the sun rises and the rain is given—and both believer and unbeliever receive their benefits—is the basis for the admonition to all of us to love our enemies and do good to those who hate us and treat us wrongfully. God's love is impartial and is demonstrated every time it rains.

2. He shows love when He disciplines us.

There is a wonderful passage in Hebrews which shows us that whenever we are disciplined, it reveals the love of God for us. When a parent truly disciplines his or her child, it is clear evidence that he or she cares about that child. Hebrews 12:5–6 quotes from an Old Testament passage (Proverbs 3:11–12) which shows that God loves the ones whom He chastens. He disciplines every son (and daughter) whom He receives. If God did not care about us, He would let us alone and allow us to ruin our lives. He cares so much that He will discipline the Christian in order that we may not destroy our testimony, victory, peace or joy. We can be thankful for His discipline when we understand that it demonstrates His love for us. He truly cares. Parents who allow their children to play in the streets when traffic is heavy, without reminding them of the danger or stopping them when they try to do it, simply do not show love for their children. If you care, you must discipline. You must reprove and correct.

3. He shows us love through the death of His Son, Jesus Christ.

Romans 5:8 teaches: "But God demonstrates His own love toward us, in that while we were still sinners, Christ died for us." We also are assured:

> In this the love of God was manifested toward us, that God has sent His only begotten Son into the world, that we might live through Him. In this is love, not that we loved God, but that He loved us and sent His Son to be the propitiation for our sins.
>
> 1 John 4:9–10

Ephesians 5:25 adds: "Christ also loved the church and gave Himself for it." The great demonstration that God truly loves us and cares about us is the fact that He sent His Son, Jesus Christ, into the world to die for our sins. God cared enough to do something about our sin problem. He truly loves us; He really cares!

4. He shows His love by sustaining us in times of trial and suffering.

God sustained the children of Israel during all the time of their wilderness wanderings. It was a great demonstration of God's love that He met their needs, even though they continued to rebel against Him. The Book of Isaiah speaks of this marvelous love of God for His people Israel, by which He sustained them through their journeys:

> I will mention the lovingkindnesses of the LORD And the praises of the LORD, According to all that the LORD has bestowed on us, And the great goodness toward the house of Israel, Which He has bestowed on them according to His mercies, According to the multitude of His lovingkind-nesses. For He said, "Surely they are My people, Children who will not lie." So He became their Savior. In all their affliction He was afflicted, And the Angel of His Presence saved them; In His love and in His pity He redeemed them; And He bore them and carried them All the days of old. But they rebelled and grieved His Holy Spirit; So He turned Himself against them as an enemy, And He fought against them.
>
> Isaiah 63:7–10

It is obvious from these verses that when Israel was afflicted, the Lord also felt that affliction. He truly cared. God cared about the people of Israel when they suffered in Egypt: ". . . their cry came up to God because of the bondage" (Exodus 2:23). "God heard their groaning" and remembered His promise to Abraham, Isaac, and Jacob (verse 24)—"and God looked upon the children of Israel, and God acknowledged them" (verse 25). God cares when we suffer; God feels our affliction deeply.

In Judges 10:16, there is a beautiful statement about God's love for His people, even in the midst of their sin and rebellion: "And His soul could no longer endure the misery of Israel."

5. He shows us His love by being patient with us.

"Love suffers long" (1 Corinthians 13:4). Longsuffering, or patience, means taking a long time to boil. It is always used with respect to persons, not objects or situations. There is a Greek word translated "patience" that refers to things and circumstances that we must endure. God is never said to be patient toward things; He does not need that kind of patience, for He is controlling all things. However, the Bible does say that God is patient toward people (2 Peter 3:9).

It is not natural to exhibit this patience; it comes from God. It is normal to be quite impatient with the way people act and respond. I found myself quite upset one day with the way a certain person was doing a job I had asked him to do. I was very impatient with him because the speed with which he was doing this task was not the speed I was demanding. I felt sick inside when I realized that my impatience was getting the best of me. When I sought God's help and confessed my sin, I noticed an immediate change in my attitude. The speed of that person no longer mattered; I was now happy that he was involved in helping me. After all, that is what really counts. I am so glad that God is patient toward us!

God had patience while Noah was building the ark (1 Peter 3:20). That generation of people deserved the judgment of God, but God was patient and gave them much opportunity to repent. After 120 years of preaching by Noah, God brought His judgment in the form of a flood upon the earth. Genesis 6:3 reminds us: "My Spirit shall not strive with man forever, for he is indeed flesh." God has great patience toward unbelievers as well as believers. He endures the wickedness and rebellion of unbelievers (Romans 9:22; 1 Peter 3:20), and He also endures the unfaithfulness and sin of believers. The words *slow to anger* in many Old Testament passages are translated into the Greek word for "longsuffering." God's patience is often connected with His forgiveness. I learn how much God loves people when I see His patience and His willingness to forgive:

> "The LORD, the LORD God, merciful and gracious, long-suffering, and abounding in goodness and truth, keeping mercy for thousands, forgiving iniquity and transgression and sin, by no means clearing the guilty, visiting the iniquity of the fathers upon the children and the children's children to the third and the fourth generation."
>
> Exodus 34:6–7

This passage clearly shows us God's patience with people and its obvious relation to forgiving our sins.

Our patience is usually tested when we run into unresponsive people. I remember well my lack of patience in dealing with a man who continued to fall back into habits of sin. Over and over again, he would seem to repent, get right with God, and then sin again. It was one discouraging cycle of events! I thought I loved him and wanted to help, but I found myself becoming more and more impatient with his sinful ways and weaknesses. I know he had a problem—but so did I! I see my problem in better focus when I think of the patience of our Lord. No matter how many times we have fallen, He is there to forgive and pick up the broken pieces. How I praise Him for His loving patience with me!

Yes, God really cares about us! His love constantly demonstrates that care. The Bible is filled with passages that teach of God's love for us. Until we really understand the dimensions of that love, the extent of that love, and the demonstration of that love, we will continue to doubt and question whether or not the God who made us cares about what we are experiencing. The more we learn, the greater comfort we have. The more we understand, the greater our assurance that He truly cares.

The Mercy of God

When we speak of mercy, we are talking about the demonstration of God's love in terms of holding back from us what we really deserve. We deserve judgment and hell because of what we have thought, said and done. But God is a God of mercy; His love makes it possible for us to be protected from the judgment we deserve. One of the great ways I feel loved and cared for by God is when I think of His mercy toward me. Deuteronomy 4:31 reminds us that He is a merciful God, and 2 Corinthians 1:3 speaks of Him as "the Father of mercies." Micah 7:18 says, "He delights in mercy." There are two major Hebrew words translated "mercy," "pity," or "compassion." The words *rachamim* and *chesed* are both found in Psalm 103:4, where we read: "Who crowns you with lovingkindness and tender mercies." *Love* describes character, what God is; *mercy* describes God's actions, what God does.

The Greatness of God's Mercy

Mercy is described in God's Word as being great and plenteous. In 1 Chronicles 21:13, David said, "I am in great distress. Please let me fall into the hand of the LORD, for His mercies are very great; but do not let me fall into the hand of man." David was very conscious of the mercy of God and how wonderful it truly is. Psalm 57:10 says, "For Your mercy reaches unto the heavens, And Your truth unto the clouds." Psalm 86:5 tells us, "For You, LORD, are good, and ready to forgive, And abundant in mercy to all those who call upon You." His mercy is abundant! His mercy is great! Psalm 89:2 adds, "Mercy shall be built up forever." And in Psalm 103:8, we read: "The LORD is merciful and gracious, Slow to anger, and abounding in mercy." Psalm 108:4 says, "For Your mercy is great above the heavens, And Your truth reaches to the clouds." Psalm 119:64 makes this tremendous claim: "The earth, O LORD, is full of Your mercy." In Psalm 136 we have this statement, *His mercy endures forever,* 26 times in 26 verses.

One of the important issues in answering the question "Does God really care?" is discovering the greatness of His mercy. Mercy extends His love to us in a special way, because it holds back from us what we really deserve. Mercy understands our weaknesses, limitations, and sins and is a demonstration that God truly cares.

How Does God Show His Mercy to Us?

In looking at the ways God demonstrates His mercy, we find our hearts being constantly encouraged. It is almost impossible not to believe that God really cares about us when we study how merciful He really is. Consider the following:

1. He shows mercy to us by not giving us what we deserve.

If God gave us what we deserve, we would be in hell. Lamentations 3:22 says, "Through the Lord's mercies we are not consumed, Because His compassions fail not." Thank the Lord that He holds back from us the judgment we deserve, because He is a merciful God! In Ephesians 2:1–3, the sinful nature and acts of man are described. We read that we are "by nature children of wrath" (verse 3), but then we find these encouraging words: "But God, who is rich in mercy, because of His great love with which He loved us" (verse 4). The words *But God* show us that there is an answer to the sinful condition of man that lies in the character of God Himself. Because He is rich in mercy, He extends salvation to us—when, in fact, we deserve the wrath of God.

2. He shows us mercy by providing for our needs when we really do not deserve it.

In Nehemiah, we have a great text demonstrating God's care for the children of Israel during their wilderness wanderings, in spite of their rebellion against Him. This text speaks of the mercies of God:

> "But they and our fathers acted proudly, Hardened their necks, And did not heed Your commandments. They refused to obey, And they were not mindful of Your wonders That You did among them. But they hardened their necks, And in their rebellion They appointed a leader To return to their bondage. But You are God, Ready to pardon, Gracious and merciful, Slow to anger, Abundant in kindness, And did not forsake them. Even when they made a molded calf for themselves, And said, 'This is your god That brought you up out of Egypt,' And worked great provocations, yet in Your manifold mercies You did not forsake them in the wilderness. The pillar of the cloud did not depart from them by day, To lead them on the road; Nor the pillar of fire by night, To show them light, And the way they should go. You also gave Your good Spirit to instruct

them, And did not withhold Your manna from their mouth,
And gave them water for their thirst. Forty years You sus-
tained them in the wilderness, So that they lacked nothing;
Their clothes did not wear out And their feet did not swell.''
Nehemiah 9:16–21

Notice carefully: *But You are God, ready to pardon, gracious
and merciful.* God makes the difference because of who He is.
Were it not for His mercies, our needs would never be met. *Yet in
Your manifold mercies You did not forsake them in the wilderness*—God led them and guided them because He is a merciful
God. He gave them food to eat and water to drink because He is
merciful. He sustained them, so that *their clothes did not wear
out and their feet did not swell.* Psalm 145:9 says: "His tender
mercies are over all His works." God's works are described as
including the giving of "food in due season. You open Your
hand And satisfy the desire of every living thing" (verses 15–
16). The reason? God is merciful to us!

3. He shows us mercy by forgiving us of our sins.

One of the great evidences of God's tender mercies toward us
is the matter of our forgiveness. He forgives all our iniquities and
crowns us "with lovingkindness and tender mercies" (Psalm
103:3–4). Verse 8 says the Lord is merciful and gracious, slow to
anger and abounding in mercy, and verse 11 tells us that His
mercy is great toward those who fear Him. The heart of the matter about forgiveness is: "As far as the east is from the west, So
far has He removed our transgressions from us" (verse 12).
That's forgiveness! Praise the Lord! His mercy has made it all
possible. God describes the exercise of His mercy in verse 13:
"As a father pities his children." He knows what we are like and
He knows that apart from His mercy, we could never be forgiven
of our sins. We have done nothing to deserve it or earn what God
offers. It is His mercy that makes it all possible. When people
ask, "Does God really care?" I turn them toward the mercy of
God.

King David learned about the mercy of God after his sin of adultery with Bathsheba. In his Prayer of Repentance, he says, "Have mercy upon me, O God, According to Your lovingkindness; According to the multitude of Your tender mercies, Blot out my transgressions" (Psalm 51:1). David understood that there is no forgiveness apart from the mercies of God. One of the great demonstrations of His great loving care for us is that He shows us mercy constantly. Were it not for His mercy, we would all perish!

God's mercies become a powerful motivation for Christian service. Paul says, "I beseech you therefore, brethren, by the mercies of God, that you present your bodies a living sacrifice, holy, acceptable to God, which is your reasonable service" (Romans 12:1). When we remember how wonderful His mercies are, we are motivated to serve Him faithfully.

One of the reasons people do not feel loved and cared for by God is the fact and presence of sin in their hearts. We will not experience the mercy of God when we attempt to hide or cover our sin. According to Proverbs 28:13: "He who covers his sins will not prosper, But whoever confesses and forsakes them will have mercy." God's mercy is given immediately to the person who confesses and forsakes his sin. Therefore, can it not be argued that when people do not feel the love and care of God for them, the root problem may be sin in their life? Sin blinds us to the love and mercy of God. It is the very mercy of God that does not punish us immediately for what we have done. It is the love and mercy of God that grants forgiveness to all who confess and forsake their sin.

God Does Care!

How could we ever doubt the loving care of God if we truly believe the Bible? As 1 Peter 5:7 says: *Casting all your care upon Him, for He cares for you.* The Bible says that HE CARES FOR YOU. We often worry about the problems in our lives, thinking that God does not care. Some of this worry is rooted in what God thinks about us and our concept of our personal worth before Him. One of the great texts that emphasizes God's care for the believer is found in Matthew, where Jesus says:

> "Therefore I say to you, do not worry about your life, what you will eat or what you will drink; nor about your body, what you will put on. Is not life more than food and the body more than clothing? Look at the birds of the air, for they neither sow nor reap nor gather into barns; yet your heavenly Father feeds them. Are you not of more value than they? Which of you by worrying can add one cubit to his stature? So why do you worry about clothing? Consider the lilies of the field, how they grow: they neither toil nor spin; and yet I say to you that even Solomon in all his glory was not arrayed like one of these. Now if God so clothes the grass of the field, which today is, and tomorrow is thrown into the oven, will He not much more clothe you, O you of little faith? Therefore do not worry, saying 'What shall we eat?' or 'What shall we drink?' or 'What shall we wear?' For after all these things the Gentiles seek. For your heavenly Father knows that you need all these things. But seek first the kingdom of God and His righteousness, and all these things shall be added to you. Therefore do not worry about tomorrow, for tomorrow will worry about its own things. Sufficient for the day is its own trouble."
>
> Matthew 6:25–34

This passage teaches that God cares about birds and flowers as well as about the believer. He knows the sparrow that falls from the tree and numbers every hair of our head. He knows about our hurts and disappointments and cares about the tears that we have shed. He is the great burden bearer who invites us to come to Him because He does care:

> For we do not have a High Priest who cannot sympathize with our weaknesses, but was in all points tempted as we are, yet without sin. Let us therefore come boldly to the throne of grace, that we may obtain mercy and find grace to help in time of need.
>
> Hebrews 4:15–16

Will God really help us? The Bible says to come to the throne of grace and you will find grace to help in your time of need. Yes, God will help—and, yes, God cares!

There is a wonderful Psalm that speaks of God's help and care:

> "I will lift up my eyes to the hills—From whence comes my help? My help comes from the LORD, Who made heaven and earth. He will not allow your foot to be moved; He who keeps you will not slumber. Behold, He who keeps Israel Shall neither slumber nor sleep. The LORD is your keeper; the LORD is your shade at your right hand. The sun shall not strike you by day, Nor the moon by night. The LORD shall preserve you from all evil; He shall preserve your soul. The LORD shall preserve your going out and your coming in From this time forth, and even forevermore."
>
> Psalm 121

This beautiful Psalm reminds us that our help comes from the Lord. It tells us that He never goes to sleep; He is watching His people constantly. It tells us that the Lord is our keeper and even our shade from the sun. It tells us that the Lord will protect us, both now and forevermore. Yes, He does care about your life and what you are going through!

"Our help is in the name of the LORD, Who made heaven and earth" (Psalm 124:8).

"As the mountains surround Jerusalem, So the LORD surrounds His people From this time forth and forever" (Psalm 125:2).

God is taking care of us because He really does care: "In the day when I cried out, You answered me, And made me bold with strength in my soul" (Psalm 138:3). God continues to care about what we feel and what we need. He is there, and He invites us to call upon Him. The Psalmist was amazed at the care of God when he wrote in Psalm 144:3–4: "LORD, what is man that You take knowledge of Him? Or the son of man, that You are mindful of him? Man is like a breath; His days are like a passing shadow."

It is a mystery to us that God cares about us. But the fact is, He does—and we rejoice in it: "The LORD is near to all who call upon Him, To all who call upon Him in truth" (Psalm 145:18). We are assured that:

> He heals the brokenhearted And binds up their wounds. He counts the number of the stars; He calls them all by name. Great is our LORD, and mighty in power; His understanding is infinite.
>
> Psalm 147:3–5

Questions to Ponder

1. Why do some people believe that God does not care?
2. How does God show His love?
3. What does mercy mean?
4. How does God show mercy to us?
5. What evidences of God's care have you seen in your life?
6. What specific problems or situations in your life need reassurance of God's love and care? What Scriptures could you use right now out of this chapter that would bring encouragement to your heart?

Bibliography

Andrews, Samuel J. *God's Revelations of Himself to Men*. New York: The Knickerbocker Press, 1901.

Bickersteth, Edward Henry. *The Trinity*. Grand Rapids: Kregel Publications, 1957.

Brown, Colin. *The New International Dictionary of New Testament Theology*, Volumes I, II, & III. Grand Rapids: Zondervan Publishing House, 1975.

Chafer, Lewis Sperry. *Systematic Theology*, Volume I. Dallas: Dallas Seminary Press, 1947.

Chapman, Colin. *Christianity on Trial*. Wheaton: Tyndale House Publishers, Inc., no date.

Chapman, Colin. *The Case for Christianity*. Grand Rapids: Wm. B. Eerdmans Publishing Co., 1981.

Charnock, Stephen. *Discourses Upon the Attributes of God*, Volumes I & II. Grand Rapids: Baker Book House, 1979.

Henry, Carl F. H. *God, Revelation, and Authority*, Volumes I–VI. Waco: Word Books, 1976.

Houston, James M. *I Believe in the Creator*. Grand Rapids: Wm. B. Eerdmans Publishing Co., 1980.

Jukes, Andrew. *The Names of God in Holy Scripture*. Grand Rapids: Kregel Publications, 1967.

Kaiser, Christopher B. *The Doctrine of God*. Westchester: Crossway Books, 1982.

Knudson, Albert C. *The Doctrine of God*. New York: The Abingdon Press, 1930.

Packer, J. *Knowing God*. Downers Grove: InterVarsity Press, 1973.

Pink, Arthur W. *The Attributes of God*. Grand Rapids: Baker Book House, 1979.

Pink, Arthur W. *The Sovereignty of God.* London: The Banner of Truth Trust, 1972.

Rosenthal, Stanley. *One God or Three?* West Collingswood: The Spearhead Press, 1978.

Schaeffer, Francis A. *The God Who Is There.* Chicago: InterVarsity Press, 1968.

Shedd, William G. T. *Dogmatic Theology,* Volume I, Grand Rapids: Zondervan Publishing House, no date.

Smail, Thomas A. *The Forgotten Father.* Grand Rapids: William B. Eerdmans Publishing Co., 1980.

Strong, Augustus Hopkins. *Systematic Theology.* Philadelphia: The Judson Press, 1907.

Sumrall, Lester. *The Names of God.* Nashville: Thomas Nelson Publishers, 1982.

Tozer, A. W. *The Knowledge of the Holy.* New York: Harper and Row Publishers, 1961.